Printed in China

Character

情操篇

陈爱明　李小艳　编译

林　立　　　审校

外文出版社

卷首语

总有一种感动无处不在。

总有一种情怀轻舞飞扬。

总有一种生活，在别处，闪动异样的光芒。

阅读，让我们的生活在情调与知性中享受更多……

故事与见闻，犹如生活的魅力与智慧，合着我们自身生命的光与影，陪伴我们一路前行。

快乐和圆满，幻想与失落，飞扬的眼泪，

行走江湖的落拓，不与人说的痛苦，渐行渐远的繁华，坚持的勇气，点点滴滴的小意思……

人生让我们感受到的，也许远远不只是这些；更多的是挫折后生长的力量，沉闷时的豁然开朗，是屋前那静静的南山上盛开的人淡如菊的境界，是闹市中跋涉红尘、豪情万丈的冲动，是很纯粹的一杯午后的香醇的咖啡……

漫步红尘，有彻悟来自他人的故事，有灵犀来自偶然的相遇，在这里，一种从未见过的却可能早就在我们心底的生活方式有可能与我们邂逅。

让我们一起阅读吧，感受生长的智慧、风雅与力量。

Contents
目　　录

One good meal deserves another
以牙还牙

When greedy Anansi took off his jacket, he floated back up to the surface of the water and hungrily watched Turtle eat his fill!

当贪婪的 Anansi 脱去夹克，他马上浮到水面上来了，只好饿着肚子看海龟吃得饱饱的。

Anansi, the Spider, hated to share! When Turtle[1] came to his house at mealtime, he said, "I can't give you food until you've washed your dusty feet!"

Turtle licked[2] his lips when he saw the big plate of steaming food, but politely walked to the stream to wash. When he returned, the plate was empty. "Good meal," Anansi said, patting his full stomach.

"One good meal deserves another!" said Turtle, "Come to my house for dinner tomorrow." Turtle fixed a fine dinner at the bottom of the river. "Come on down and eat!" he said.

Anansi filled his jacket pockets with stones so that he would be weighted down enough to stay at the river's bottom and eat. "It's impolite to wear a jacket to dinner!" Turtle said, "Take it off!"

But when greedy[3] Anansi took off his jacket, he floated[4] back up to the surface of the water and hungrily watched Turtle eat his fill[5]!

蜘蛛 Anansi 不喜欢和别人分享东西。当海龟在吃饭时间来到他家时，他说："你去把你的脏脚洗了才能吃我的饭！"

海龟看到一大盘热气腾腾的食物，舔了舔嘴唇，但还是很礼貌地走到小溪边去洗脚。当他回来时，盘子已经空了。"真好吃！" Anansi 拍着他圆滚滚的肚子说。

"我要以牙还牙！"海龟说，"明天来我家吃饭吧。"海龟在河底准备了一顿丰盛的晚餐。"下来吃吧！"他说。

Anansi 把夹克口袋里装满石头，使他能够沉到河底去吃。"穿着夹克吃饭是不礼貌的。"海龟说，"脱了吧！"

但是当贪婪的 Anansi 脱去夹克，他马上浮到水面上来了，只好饿着肚子看海龟吃得饱饱的。

❶ turtle /ˈtɜːtl/
n. 海龟
❷ lick /lɪk/
v. 舔
❸ greedy
/ˈɡriːdɪ/
adj. 贪婪的
❹ float /fləʊt/
v. 漂
❺ eat one's fill
吃得饱饱的

An ant and a grasshopper

蚂蚁和蚱蜢

Don't keep on working hard with no direction.

不要没有方向地拼命工作。

Once upon a time, there lived an ant and a grasshopper[1]. The grasshopper did nothing else but jumped around and played.

On the other hand, the ant was so hardworking, looking for food all day long and stored[2] them in its nest.

Looking at his hardworking friend working so hard, the grasshopper asked, "Hey, Ant! You don't have to relax[3]? Always busy one. Come and play with me."

To that the ant replied, "I can't relax. I have to store all the food."

"Well! Relax. Why you bother storing all the food? When you are hungry just go and find some food," the grasshopper told the ant again.

"Eh, I cannot relax. I have to standby for the coming winter season. Then I don't need to panic. I think you also must stand-by," the ant telling his friend. "When I get time, I go and play. If you want to store food, you go ahead. I continue playing ok ... bye!" And hop went the grasshopper.

The ant was a hardworking guy ... oops I mean insect. Not like the grasshopper who was so lazy. And so as days, weeks, months went by, the winter still has not come yet but the ant was still seen searching and storing food.

从前有一只蚂蚁和一只蚱蜢。蚱蜢什么事也不做，只是四处跳跃、玩耍。而蚂蚁却整天辛勤工作，寻找食物，储藏在巢里。

看到勤奋的朋友工作得这么卖力，蚱蜢问："嗨，蚂蚁，你总是这么忙，都不休息一下吗？快来和我一块玩吧！"

蚂蚁回答道："我不能休息，我必须要储存食物呢。"

蚱蜢又说："休息一会吧，为什么总是忙着储存食物呢？当你饿的时候就去找一些食物得了。"

"呃，我不能休息。冬天快要来了，我必须要做好准备，到时候我就不会发愁。我觉得你也应该做好准备。"蚂蚁告诉他的朋友说。"有空的时候我就去玩。你要储存食物随便你。我要继续去玩了，再见！"说着蚱蜢一蹦一跳地走了。

蚂蚁是一个勤奋的小伙子，哦，应该是昆虫。它不像蚱蜢那么懒。时间一天一天，一星期一星期，一个月一个月地流逝，冬天还没来，蚂蚁却还在四处寻找储存食物。

这两个朋友又碰巧遇到了。"嗨，蚂蚁，你还没储存完呀？上次的食物哪去了？这么快就吃完啦？"蚱蜢问道。

"我储存得太多，因为冬天还没到，都

❶ grasshopper
/ˈɡrɑːsˌhɒpə(r)/
n. 蚱蜢
❷ store
/stɔː(r)/
v. 储存
❸ relax
/rɪˈlæks/
v. 放松

The two friends happened to meet again. "Hey Ant! You still haven't finished storing food, ah? Last time where did all the food go? So fast finish, ah?" asked grasshopper.

"I got keep but all overdue[4]. So cannot eat anymore. All because winter not here yet. Now I have to go and look for new food," sighed the ant.

"But ant, you don't mind if I ask you? Did you ever have a thought that Singapore and Malaysia where got winter?" asked the grasshopper again. "AHHHH????!!!!!" The ant was shocked!

The moral of the story is whatever you do better think properly first. Sometimes we go too busily in life and follow our routine[5] too tightly but most importantly, work towards where you want to go in your life, what is it that you want, what is it that you REALLY want, what's your dream, is what you are doing now moving towards your dream?

If it's not, don't just keep on working hard only just because someone in your life told you that this is the way and just because everyone is doing it!!

Don't keep on working hard with no direction[6]. Focus on the direction of your life, not your work but your life. Plan your life.

已经过期，不能吃了。现在我必须要去寻找
新的食物了!"蚂蚁叹气说。

"蚂蚁，你不介意我问你一个问题吧，
你想过新加坡和马来西亚有冬天吗?"蟑螂
又问道。"啊???!!!"蚂蚁很吃惊。

这则故事的寓意就是三思而后行。有时
生活太匆忙，太遵循日常惯例。但是最重要
的是在你的生命中，你工作是想达到什么目
的，你想要什么，你真正想要的是什么，你
的梦想是什么，你现在所做的是为了实现你
的梦想吗?

如果不是，那就不要仅仅是因为你生命
中的其他人告诉你生活就是这样，或者仅仅
是因为每个人都拼命地工作，你也就只顾拼
命地工作。

不要没有方向地拼命工作。重点是要把
握住你生活的方向，不是工作而是生活的方
向。计划好你的生活吧!

④ **overdue**
/ˌəʊvəˈdjuː/
adj. 过期的
⑤ **routine**
/ruːˈtiːn/
n. 日常例惯
⑥ **direction**
/dɪˈrekʃən/
n. 方向

Our problem

我们的问题

Remember that when anyone of us is in trouble, we are all at risk.

记住，我们中任何一个人遇到麻烦，我们都处于危险之中。

A little mouse living on a farm was looking through a crack in the wall one day and saw the farmer and his wife opening a package.

The mouse was intrigued[1] by what food the package may contain. He was aghast[2] to discover that it was a mousetrap. The mouse ran to the farmyard warning everyone "there is a mousetrap in the house, there is a mouse trap in the house."

The chicken raised his head and said, "Mr. Mouse, I can tell you this trap is a grave[3] concern to you, but it has no consequence to me and I cannot be bothered with it."

The mouse turned to the pig, "I am so sorry Mr. Mouse, but the trap is no concern of mine either!"

The mouse then turned to the bull, "It sounds like you have a problem Mr. Mouse, but not one that concerns me."

The mouse returned to the house, head down and dejected[4] that no one would help him or has concerned about his dilemma.

He knew he had to face the trap on his own. That night the sound of a trap catching its prey[5] was heard throughout the house. The farmer's wife rushed to see what was caught. In the darkness she could not see that it was a venomous[6] snake whose tail the trap had caught.

一天，一只住在农场的小老鼠透过墙上的洞看到农场主和他的妻子打开了一个包裹。

小老鼠很好奇里面装的是什么好吃的食物，但是令它震惊的是，里面居然是一个老鼠夹。于是它跑到农场的院子里向每一个人警告说："屋里有一个老鼠夹！屋里有一个老鼠夹！"

一只小鸡抬起头说："老鼠先生，我敢说老鼠夹是专为你设置的，不会给我带来任何后果，我用不着担心。"

老鼠转向猪。"我也很抱歉，老鼠先生，老鼠夹和我也没有任何关系。"

老鼠又去跟牛讲。"听起来你好像遇到了麻烦，老鼠先生，但是这也不关我的事。"

老鼠耷拉着脑袋回到屋子里，他感到很沮丧，因为没有一个人愿意帮助它，没有一个人为它的困境担心。

它只有独自面对这个老鼠夹了。那天晚上整间屋子都听到了夹子夹住东西的声音。农夫的妻子急忙跑过去看是什么被抓住了，黑暗中她看不清是一条毒蛇的尾巴被夹住了。

农夫的妻子被毒蛇咬了一口，发起了高烧。农夫知道最好的退烧办法是喝鸡汤，于是他拿着菜刀走进院子去取做汤的原料。

❶ intrigue
/ɪnˈtriːg/
v. 激起好奇心

❷ aghast
/əˈgɑːst/
adj. 惊恐的

❸ grave /greɪv/
adj. 严峻的

❹ dejected
/dɪˈdʒektɪd/
adj. 沮丧的

❺ prey /preɪ/
n. 捕获物

❻ venomous
/ˈvenəməs/
adj. 有毒的

The snake bit the farmer's wife. The wife caught a bad fever and the farmer knew the best way to treat a fever was with chicken soup. The farmer took his hatchet[7] to the farmyard to get the soup's main ingredient[8].

The wife got sicker and friends and neighbors came by to take turns sitting with her round the clock. The farmer knew he had to feed them, so he butchered the pig.

The farmer's wife did not get better, in fact she died and so many friends and family came to her funeral that the farmer had to slaughter[9] the bull to feed all of them.

So the next time we hear that one of our teammates is facing a problem and think it does not concern or effect us, let us remember that when anyone of us is in trouble, we are all at risk.

Life is a celebration. Be happy and make others happy.

农夫的妻子病得更重了，朋友和邻居们全天轮流来看她。农夫必须招待他们，所以就把猪杀了。

农夫的妻子还是没有好转，后来死了，很多朋友和家人来参加她的葬礼，农夫只有杀了牛来招待他们。

所以，下一次我们听到我们当中的一员遇到问题时，不要想这不关我们的事，不会影响我们，记住，我们中任何一个人遇到麻烦，我们都处于危险之中。

生活就是联欢，高兴一点，让其他人也高兴起来！

❼ hatchet
/'hætʃɪt/
n. 短柄小斧

❽ ingredient
/ɪn'griːdjənt/
n. (烹调的)原料

❾ slaughter
/'slɔːtə(r)/
v. 屠杀

The city mouse and the country mouse
城里老鼠和乡下老鼠

Thank you, but I'll take my humble crumbs in comfort over all of your finery with fear!

谢谢你，你心惊胆战地在这吃你的美味佳肴，我还是回去心安理得地吃我的低级面包屑吧。

There once was a mouse that liked his country house until his cousin[1] came for a visit.

"In the city where I live," his cousin said, "we dine on cheese and fish and bread. Each night my dinner is brought to me. I eat whatever I choose. While you, country cousin, work your paws to the bone for humble[2] crumbs[3] in this humble home. I'm used to finery[4]. To each my own, I see!"

Upon hearing this, the country mouse looked again at his plain brown house. Suddenly he wasn't satisfied anymore. "Why should I hunt and scrape[5] for food to store?" he said, "Cousin, I'm coming to the city with you!"

Off they went into the fine town house of the plump and prosperous city mouse.

"Shhh! The people are in the parlor[6]," the city mouse said, "Let's sneak into the kitchen for some cheese and bread."

The city mouse gave his wide-eyed country cousin a grand tour of the leftover food on the table. "It's the easy life," the city mouse said, and he smiled as he bit into a piece of bread.

Just as they were both about to bite into a chunk of [7] cheddar[8] cheese, in came the CAT!

"Run! Run!" said the city mouse, "The cat's in the house!"

从前，乡下有一只老鼠，在它表兄来看它之前，一直都很喜欢它的房子。

"在我住的城市里，"它的表兄说，"我们吃奶酪、鱼、面包。每天晚上我面前都放着好多食物，我爱吃什么就吃什么。而你，乡下的老弟，却在这个简陋的屋子里卖力寻找次等的面包屑。我已经习惯过高贵优雅的生活了，习惯房屋里的一切。"

听到这，乡下老鼠又看看他简陋的褐色房子，突然它再也不满足了。"为什么我要寻找，要一点点地收集食物呢?"它说，"表兄，我想和你去城里。"

于是它们出发到这个圆滚滚的应有尽有的城市老鼠的家里去了。

"嘘! 有人在客厅。"城里老鼠说，"我们偷偷地溜到厨房找一些奶酪和面包吧。"

城里老鼠把大开了眼界的乡下老鼠带到一大桌子剩菜剩饭前。"瞧，生活多舒适!"城里老鼠说，咬了一片面包笑了。

正当它们两个要咬一大块美国奶酪时，竟然进来了一只猫!

"快跑! 快跑!"城里老鼠说，"屋子里有猫!"

当乡下老鼠跳出窗外逃命时，它说: "表兄，我要回乡下去。你从来没有告诉我有猫住

① **cousin**
/ˈkʌzən/
n. 表兄

② **humble**
/ˈhʌmbl/
adj. 低劣的简陋的

③ **crumb** /krʌm/
n. 面包屑

④ **finery**
/ˈfaɪnəri/
n. 高贵，优雅

⑤ **scrape** /skreɪp/
v. 刮，擦

⑥ **parlor** /ˈpɑːlə/
n. 客厅

⑦ **a chunk of**
一大块

⑧ **cheddar**
/ˈtʃedə(r)/
n. 美国干酪

Just as the country mouse scampered[9] for his life out of the window, he said, "Cousin, I'm going back to the country! You never told me that a CAT lives here! Thank you, but I'll take my humble crumbs in comfort over all of your finery with fear!"

在这儿。谢谢你，你心惊胆战地在这吃你的
美味佳肴，我还是回去心安理得地吃我的低
级面包屑吧。"

The purse of gold
金钱包

I believe you both. Justice is possible!

我相信你们两个人, 还是公断地处理吧!

A beggar found a leather[1] purse that someone had dropped in the marketplace[2]. Opening it, he discovered that it contained 100 pieces of gold. Then he heard a merchant shout, "A reward[3]! A reward to the one who finds my leather purse!"

Being an honest man, the beggar came forward and handed the purse to the merchant saying, "Here is your purse. May I have the reward now?"

"Reward?" scoffed[4] the merchant, greedily counting his gold. "Why, the purse I dropped had 200 pieces of gold in it. You've already stolen more than the reward! Go away or I'll tell the police."

"I'm an honest man," said the beggar defiantly[5], "Let us take this matter to the court."

In court the judge patiently listened to both sides of the story and said, "I believe you both. Justice is possible! Merchant, you stated that the purse you lost contained 200 pieces of gold. Well, that's a considerable cost. But, the purse this beggar found had only 100 pieces of gold. Therefore, it couldn't be the one you lost."

And, with that, the judge gave the purse and all the gold to the beggar.

一个乞丐在集市发现了一个别人丢失的皮钱包。他打开一看，发现里面有100条金子。突然他听到一个商人大声叫喊："有重谢啊！谁发现我的皮钱包谁有重谢啊！"

乞丐很诚实，走过去把钱包递给商人说："这是你的钱包吧，我现在可以得到重谢了吗？"

"重谢？"商人嘲讽地说，贪婪地数他的金子，"哼，我丢失的钱包里有200条金子，你偷的金子比我要重谢的还要多。走开，不然我要叫警察了！"

"我很诚实！"乞丐不服，"我们到法庭评理去！"

法庭上法官耐心地听完两个人讲的经过后说："我相信你们两个人，还是公断地处理吧！商人，你说你丢失的钱包里有200条金子，这真是一大笔钱。但是这个乞丐发现的钱包里只有100条金子，因此，这个钱包不是你丢的那一个。"

说完之后，法官把这个钱包和所有的钱都给了乞丐。

❶ **leather**
/ˈleðə(r)/
n. 皮革
❷ **marketplace**
/ˈmɑːkɪtpleɪs/
n. 集市
❸ **reward**
/rɪˈwɔːd/
n. 奖赏
❹ **scoff** /skɒf/
v. 嘲笑
❺ **defiantly**
/diˈfaɪəntlɪ/
adv. 对抗地

The lion and the mouse

狮子和老鼠

Dear friend, I was foolish to ridicule you for being small.

亲爱的朋友，我嘲笑你太小真是太傻了。

A small mouse crept[1] up to a sleeping lion. The mouse admired the lion's ears, his long whiskers[2] and his great mane.

"Since he's sleeping," thought the mouse, "he'll never suspect[3] I'm here!"

With that, the little mouse climbed up onto the lion's tail, ran across its back, slid[4] down its leg and jumped off of its paw[5]. The lion awoke and quickly caught the mouse between its claws[6].

"Please," said the mouse, "let me go and I'll come back and help you someday."

The lion laughed, "You are so small! How could ever help me?"

The lion laughed so hard he had to hold his belly! The mouse jumped to freedom and ran until she was far, far away.

The next day, two hunters came to the jungle. They went to the lion's lair[7]. They set a huge rope snare. When the lion came home that night, he stepped into the trap.

He roared! He wept! But he couldn't pull himself free.

The mouse heard the lion's pitiful roar and came back to help him.

一只小老鼠一声不响地走近一头睡熟的狮子。小老鼠很羡慕狮子的耳朵，长长的胡须，还有威风的鬃毛。

"既然它睡着了，"小老鼠想，"它肯定不会知道我在这的！"

带着这种想法，小老鼠爬上了狮子的尾巴，穿过它的背，顺着腿滑下去。跳下狮爪时，狮子醒了，迅速抓住了老鼠。

"求求你，"老鼠说，"放了我吧，有一天我会回来帮你的。"

狮子笑了，"你这么小，怎么帮我？"

狮子笑得直捂肚子。老鼠趁机跳走，获得自由了，它跑得很远很远。

第二天，两个猎人来到丛林，走向狮子的洞穴。他们用一个特大的绳网做陷阱。狮子那天晚上回家时，掉进去了。

它大叫，大哭，但是还是逃不出去。

小老鼠听到了狮子可怜的叫喊声，回来帮它。

小老鼠看了看陷阱，注意到了收紧网的粗绳。它开始咬啊咬，最后把绳子咬断了。狮子抖落其它的绳子，又获得了自由。

狮子转向小老鼠说："亲爱的朋友，我

❶ creep /kriːp/
v.蹑蹑脚地走
❷ whisker
/ˈwɪskə(r)/
n. 胡须
❸ suspect
/səˈspekt/
v. 怀疑
❹ slide /slaɪd/
v. 滑行
❺ paw /pɔː/
n.（狮子、狗、猫等四足动物的）爪子
❻ claw /klɔː/
n.（鸟、兽、昆虫等的）爪子
❼ lair /leə(r)/
n. 洞穴

The mouse eyed the trap and noticed the one thick rope that held it together. She began nibbling[8] and nibbling until the rope broke. The lion was able to shake off the other ropes that held him tight. He stood up free again!

The lion turned to the mouse and said, "Dear friend, I was foolish to ridicule[9] you for being small. You helped me by saving my life after all!"

嘲笑你太小真是太傻了。是你最后帮了我，救了我的命。"

Playground — the sacred and unpolluted plot in my mind

操场
我心中神圣纯净的地方

I enjoy the tranquil time belonging to me in my inner heart, with all my heart and soul.

我全身心地享受着属于我的内心宁静的时刻。

I love playground, not only because it has always been the cradle of training and fostering[1] excellent athletes for hundred and thousand years, but also because it consistently provides place and space for the common people like me to do physical exercises in, then we can have a strong body.

But to me, it is preferable to be my spirit home, where I could let off[2] dissatisfied moods, adjust and relax myself. The most important of all,　it's a wonderful place for me to generate new thoughts. To some writers, maybe the toilet is the right place to have new thoughts. The meaning of the playground to me is just like Mecca[3], the sacred place, to the Muslim[4].

The function I said about the playground seems a little exaggerating, but it works on me, indeed.

When I am not in good mood, I find a playground, if it is not too far from me, then sitting quietly at a corner of it. There may be no person,　or just one or two pairs of lovers are walking slowly, but all that won't affect me, all I need to do is sitting there, just sitting. I enjoy the tranquil[5] time belonging to me in my inner heart, with all my heart and soul. Nothing needed to worry about, nothing needed to think of, only let my soul wandering through the vast and tremendous space, crossing through the endless cosmos[6], from time to time, it could land on some weird[7] and mysterious planet, meeting some odd[8] extraterrestrials[9] (ET), but there's no necessity for me to say "hi" to them, they probably can't understand the most ordinary greeting word on our home land—the

我喜欢操场，不仅是因为千百年来它是训练、培养优秀运动员的摇篮，还因为它总是给像我这样的普通人提供锻炼身体的地方，使我们能有强健的体魄。

但是它对我来说更是精神的家园。我可以在那释放我的不满情绪，调整放松自己，最重要的是，它更能激发我的新思想。对一些作家来说，可能厕所正是他们产生灵感的地方。操场对于我的意义就像麦加对于穆斯林一样，是个神圣的地方。

我所说的操场的作用似乎有点夸张，但是它的确对我大有意义。

当我心情不好的时候，我就找个操场，如果操场不远的话。我静静地坐在操场的一角。没有一个人，或者仅仅有一两对情侣在慢慢地散步，但他们都不会影响我。我只需要坐在那儿，只是坐着。我全身心地享受着属于我的内心宁静的时刻。什么也不用担心，什么也不用想，只是放飞我的思绪飞向广阔无垠的太空，穿过无尽的宇宙，有时着陆在某个奇异的神秘的行星上，遇到一些古怪的外星人，而不用和他们打招呼，因为他们可能不会明白在我们的家园——地球上——最平常的问候。如果在他们的星球上，微笑、大笑也代表友谊、和平、友好的

❶ foster
/ˈfɒstə(r)/
n. 培养，抚育

❷ let off
释放

❸ Mecca
/ˈmekə/
n. 麦加

❹ Muslim
/ˈmʊzlɪm/
n. 穆斯林

❺ tranquil
/ˈtræŋkwɪl/
adj. 宁静的

❻ cosmos
/ˈkɒzmɒs/
n. 宇宙

❼ weird
/wɪəd/
adj. 奇异的

❽ odd
/ɒd/
adj. 古怪的

❾ extraterrestrial
/ˌekstrətɪˈrestrɪəl/
n. 外星人

earth; a simple smile is ok, I think, if the smile or laugh also rep-
resent friendship, peace, kindness in their planet.

But I won't allow my thought drift too far like a wild horse escaping from the rope tied to it. Having finished my fantastic spirit
trip, I feel much better, and all of a sudden I feel everything by my
side is so beautiful, simply I haven't noticed and found their beau-
ties and magic.

Such so-called difficulties I have encountered and I will meet,
is nothing but small theatrical[9] interlude[10] which is inevitable in everybody's life. Only if I have correct attitudes at it, all the unhappy, even sorrow and tears of sad will go with the wind.

At last, the point I want to mention to you is that I write this es-
say in an anonymous small-sized playground, which locates vicinity[11] to my home.

话，我想一个简单的微笑就足够了。

但是我不会让思绪像一匹脱了缰的野马一样跑得很远。完成我奇妙的精神旅途后，我感觉好多了。我突然发现身边的一切都这么美好，只是我没有注意和发现他们的美妙和魅力罢了。

我所遇到的和将要遇到的所谓困难仅仅是生命中小小的戏剧插曲，这些困难在每个人的生命中都不可避免。只有我保持积极的态度，所有的不幸、痛苦和伤心的眼泪才会随风飘散。

最后我要告诉你的是，我是在我家附近的一个不知名的小操场上写下这篇短文的。

⑩ **theatrical**
/θɪˈætrɪkəl/
adj. 戏剧的
⑪ **interlude**
/ˈɪntəluːd/
n. 插曲
⑫ **vicinity**
/vɪˈsɪnətɪ/
n. 邻近, 附近

Good and evil have just rewards

善有善报,恶有恶报

It seems that one thought can determine one's fate. It all depends on whether that thought is good or evil.

一个人的想法似乎能决定一个人的命运,这完全取决于这个想法是善良的还是邪恶的。

It's hard to imagine what one would think about just as one is unexpectedly faced with death; but the thought at that moment determines[1] one's fate.

There is a story in Buddhism: in the past, a person named Gan Daduo committed[2] all manner of crimes. One day while he was walking on a street, he saw that he was about to step on a spider. A kind thought came to him: "A spider is a small life, but why should I kill it?" So he stepped over the spider and avoided killing it.

Since he had done so many bad things, he fell into an endless hell when he died. While he was suffering, a silver thread[3] from a spider fell down from the sky. Feeling as if he had found a boat after falling into the sea, he quickly climbed up the thread with his all strength to escape from the pains of hell. But as he was climbing, he looked down and saw many other sentient[4] beings were also climbing up after him. He was afraid that the fine thread could not stand so much weight and would break, ruining his chance to escape. He kicked down all of the others one after another. But as he was kicking his companions, the spider thread broke, and Gan Daduo and all the sentient beings fell into hell again to suffer in endless misery.

His earlier kind thought had given Gan Daduo a chance to escape from hell; but his bad thought had drawn him back to hell to suffer again. It seems that one thought can determine one's fate. It all depends on whether that thought is good or evil.

很难想像当一个人突然面临死亡的时候会怎么想，但是他在那个时候的想法却决定他的命运。

佛教里有一个故事：从前，有一个叫甘大多的人做尽了坏事。一天他在街上走，看见自己正要踩到一只蜘蛛时，脑子里突然闪过一个善良的想法：一只蜘蛛，这么小的生命，我为什么要踩死它呢？于是他就抬起脚迈了过去，没有踩死它。

因为他做了那么多坏事，所以死后掉进了深不见底的地狱。当他饱受折磨时，蜘蛛的一根银丝从天上掉下来，他感觉就像是落入大海找到了一条救生船，使出全身力气迅速地沿着这根丝往上爬，逃离痛苦的地狱，但是当他爬的时候，他往下一看，发现很多其他有知觉的人也随着他往上爬。他很害怕细线承受不了这么大的重量而断掉，毁了他逃生的机会，于是他把那些人一个个踢下去。但是当他踢他的同伴时，蜘蛛丝断开了。甘大多和所有的人又跌入了无边的苦难。

甘大多先前的善心给了他一个逃离地狱的机会，但是他的恶意又把他拽回地狱受苦。一个人的想法似乎能决定一个人的命运，这完全取决于这个想法是善良的还是邪恶的。

❶ determine
/dɪˈtɜːmɪn/
v. 决定

❷ commit
/kəˈmɪt/
v. 做（错事）；犯（罪）

❸ thread
/θred/
n. 线，丝

❹ sentient
/ˈsenʃɪənt/
adj. 有知觉的

A boy and a king

小孩和国王

Here my God remains with me through twenty four hours and looks after me when I am asleep.

在这儿，上帝24小时和我在一起，在我睡着的时候照看我。

Once a king set out on his horse to visit the city he ruled.

As he was going around the city he saw a very unusual sight. He saw a little boy on the road who was playing with mud and dust. As the king looked at the boy he saw something that struck him immediately. He understood that this was not an ordinary boy. He had a mystic[1] look in his eyes and the king was curious to know more about him.

The king called the boy to his side and asked him as to why he was playing with mud and dust. The boy with his piercing[2] eyes looked at the king and asked him who he was.

The king answered that he was the king of that country and repeated the same question to the boy as to why he was playing with mud and dust. The boy without looking up at the king continued playing and said, "This human body is made up of mud and dust and ultimately is going to mingle[3] in that only. Therefore I am playing with it because I am made from it. O mighty king now you tell me what else should I play with."

The king had no answer to such a profound[4] question and did not know what to say in reply to such a little boy. He immediately realized that he was not an ordinary human being. Therefore he asked the boy to accompany[5] him to his palace and stay with him for the rest of his life. The boy said, "O mighty king, I am willing to live in your palace if you can fulfill my two conditions. First, you have to be with me through all twenty four hours and second, you

从前，一个国王骑马出去参观他统治的城市。

当他在城里四处看时，看到一个奇怪的景象：一个小男孩在路边玩泥土。国王看着他，立即被他吸引了。他知道这不是一个普通的小男孩，因为小男孩的目光很神秘。国王很好奇，想更多的了解他。

国王把小男孩叫到身边问他为什么玩泥土。小男孩用锐利的目光看着国王，问他是谁。

国王回答说他是这个国家的国王，又问小男孩同样的问题：为什么玩泥土？小男孩头也没抬，边玩边说："人的身体是由泥土做的，最终也将融入泥土。我玩泥土是因为我是由它做成的。国王陛下，你能告诉我还能玩什么吗？"

国王不能回答这个深刻的问题，也不知道应该对这样一个小男孩说什么。他立刻意识到他不是一个普通人，因此他叫小男孩和他一起回宫，一辈子和他住在一起。小男孩说："国王陛下，如果你能满足我两个条件，我就和你住在宫殿。第一，你必须24小时和我在一起；第二，当我睡着的时候，你不能睡觉。"

国王有点吃惊，他说："好的，我可以

① mystic
/ˈmɪstɪk/
adj. 神秘的

② piercing
/ˈpɪəsɪŋ/
adj. 锐利的

③ mingle
/ˈmɪŋɡl/
v. 结合，混合

④ profound
/prəʊˈfaʊnd/
adj. 深远的，深刻的

⑤ accompany
/əˈkʌmpənɪ/
v. 伴随，陪伴

have to remain awake when I am asleep."

The king was slightly startled. He said, "Alright, I shall remain with you for all twenty four hours. But I shall not keep awake when you are asleep."

The boy at once jumped up to his feet, saluted him and said, "In that case I cannot go with you to your palace. Here my God remains with me through twenty four hours and looks after me when I am asleep. I am not a fool to leave my God and come with you. O mighty king, thank you and goodbye."

Saying that the boy went his way.

The king was dumbfounded[6] and had nothing to say to the divine[7] boy.

What a great little boy!

What a little great king!

和你 24 小时在一起，但是在你睡觉时我不能不睡觉。"

小男孩立即站了起来，向他敬礼说："那样的话，我就不能和你回宫了。在这儿，上帝 24 小时和我在一起，在我睡着的时候照看我。我不是傻瓜，离开我的上帝跟你走。国王陛下，谢谢，再见!"

说着，小男孩径自走开了。

国王目瞪口呆，对着那个圣孩说不出一句话。

多么伟大的小男孩!

多么渺小的尊贵国王!

❻ dumbfound
/dʌmˈfaʊnd/
v. 惊呆

❼ divine
/diˈvaɪn/
adj. 神灵的

The jackal king

胡狼国王

One should never try to put on fake masks for sooner or later you will be discovered.

一个人永远不要戴假面具，因为迟早是要曝光的。

Once upon a time, many animals lived together in a dense jungle. The king of the jungle was the mighty and majestic lion. Every animal bowed its head before the mighty lion king. The jungle was full of many different kinds of animals like tigers, bears, leopards[1] and even jackals[2].

One day a jackal was very hungry and was not able to procure[3] any food for himself for number of days. He became completely emaciated[4] and looked skinnier than other jackals. Soon it became difficult even to recognize him. Finally when he could not bear his hunger pangs[5] any more he decided to look for some food in the nearby town.

The dogs saw him going towards the town and started running after him. The jackal sensing danger, decide to hide himself in a drum which was full of blue paint. After the dogs went away the jackal came out of the drum but now his body had turned blue. He went to the nearby pond to quench[6] his thirst and saw his blue color. The jackal was horrified. While he was drinking water from the pond some other animals of the jungle saw him. They could not recognize him and were frightened and hence immediately ran away. The jackal being a crafty[7] and cunning[8] animal soon realized that other animals were frightened of him. He decided to take advantage of his disguise. He called all animals of the jungle and thundered in front of them, " Hey, you fools, do you know who I am?" All animals were cold with fear. The lion, however mustered[9] some courage and fumbled[10], "No my lord, your majesty seems to have been sent by God in heaven to rule us and we re-

从前，有很多动物住在茂密的丛林里，丛林的国王是威严的狮子，每一个动物在威严的狮子王面前都要低头敬礼。丛林里有各种各样的动物，老虎、熊、豹甚至还有胡狼。

一天，一只饥饿的胡狼好几天都没弄到东西吃了。它日渐衰弱，看上去比其它胡狼更瘦。不久，连认出它都很难了。最后，它再也忍受不了饥饿的痛苦，决定到附近的城镇去寻找食物。

狗看到它朝城镇走来，开始追着它叫。胡狼意识到有危险，决定藏到一个装满蓝色涂料的鼓形大容器里。等狗走了之后它才出来，但现在它浑身都变成了蓝色。它到附近的池塘去喝水解渴时看到身上的蓝色非常恐惧。丛林里的其它动物看到它在那儿喝水，没认出是它来，都非常害怕，立即跑开了。狡猾奸诈的胡狼马上意识到其它动物都被他吓着了，它决定利用这个伪装。它把丛林里的动物都叫来，大声对它们说："你们这些傻瓜知道我是谁吗？"所有的动物都吓得直打冷颤。但是狮子鼓起勇气笨拙地说："我们不知道，大王。你真威武，好像是天堂的上帝派来统治我们的，我们要求你来保护我们。请你从我手里拿走统治的权利吧。"其

❶ **leopard**
/ˈlepəd/
n. 豹

❷ **jackal**
/ˈdʒækɔːl/
n. 胡狼

❸ **procure**
/prəʊˈkjʊə(r)/
v. 获得

❹ **emaciated**
/ɪˈmeɪsɪeɪtɪd/
adj. 瘦弱的，憔悴的

❺ **pang** /pæŋ/
n. 痛苦

❻ **quench**
/kwentʃ/
v. 消除；抑制

❼ **crafty**
/ˈkrɑːftɪ/
adj. 狡猾的

❽ **cunning**
/ˈkʌnɪŋ/
adj. 奸诈的

❾ **muster**
/ˈmʌstə(r)/
v. 鼓起(勇气等)

❿ **fumble**
/ˈfʌmbl/
v. 笨拙地说

quest you to protect us and take the reins of the jungle from me."
Other animals at once consented and said in unison[11], "Yes, yes,
you are our Lord and please take the reins from the lion and
oblige us." The cunning jackal nodded and accepted obligingly.

He was however worried about his brethren[12], the other jackals of the jungle. So he asked the lion and tiger to drive all jackals
away from the jungle. The lion and tiger did accordingly and soon
all jackals were banished from the jungle.

Now the jackal was never hungry. All other animals of the jungle served him with the best available food. He became fat once
again and was enjoying his newly gained power. Every animal in
the jungle feared him and obeyed him. The jackal couldn't have
asked for anything more. Other animals tried to figure out who their
new king was but they couldn't come to any conclusion.

On one full moon night, a few banished jackals who had hid-
den themselves, started howling as all jackals do on full moon
night.

This jackal too could not control himself and started howling
with other jackals. The secret was out and all animals in the jungle
discovered his real identity.

The lions, tigers and bears at once pounced[13] on the jackal
and ate him up. Thus came the cruel end of cunning and scheming[14]
jackal. The lion once again became the king of the jungle and ev-

它动物也立即同意，附和道："是的，你是我们的上帝，请从狮子手里拿走权力统治我们吧！"狡猾的胡狼点点头，迫不及待的接受了。

然而，它还是担心它的同伙——丛林里的其它胡狼，于是它让狮子和老虎把所有的胡狼都赶出丛林。狮子和老虎照做了，于是所有的胡狼都被赶出了丛林。

现在，胡狼再也不用挨饿了，丛林里的所有其它的动物把所能找到的食物都献给它吃。它又一次胖了起来，享受它新获得的权力。丛林里的每一个动物都害怕它、服从它，能给的都给它。其它动物想办法辨认它们的新国王到底是谁，但是它们都没有得出任何结论。

一个满月的晚上，一些在被驱逐时躲藏起来的胡狼开始嚎叫。所有的胡狼在满月的晚上都要嚎叫。

这只胡狼忍不住也和其它胡狼一起嚎叫。于是，秘密暴露了，丛林里的所有动物都发现了它的真实身份。

狮子、老虎、熊马上向胡狼扑去，把它吃掉了。这就是狡猾的、诡计多端的胡狼的悲惨结局。狮子又当上了丛林的国王，所有的动物又融洽地在一起生活。

⑪ **unison**
/ˈjuːnɪzən/
n. 一致
⑫ **brethren**
/ˈbreðrən/
n. 成员，同志
⑬ **pounce**
/paʊns/
v. 突然扑向
⑭ **scheming**
/ˈskiːmɪŋ/
adj. 诡计多端的

eryone lived in harmony in the jungle once again.

The moral of the story is that it is very difficult to put on a fade for a long time. The jackal used his crafty ways to become the king of jungle but he could not help his real nature and hence was soon discovered. One should never try to put on fake masks for sooner or later you will be discovered. So it is important that we remain who we are and then try to bring about positive[15] changes in ourselves.

这个故事的寓意是：伪装长不了。胡狼用狡猾的手段当上了丛林的国王，但是它的掩盖不了自己真实的本性，因此身份很快就暴露了。一个人永远不要戴假面具，因为迟早是要曝光的。所以保持自我，并尽力完善自己很重要。

⓯ positive
/ˈpɒzətɪv/
adj. 积极的

Honesty

诚　实

Whenever a man lies, it is for a good and honorable reason, and for the benefit of others.

当一个人撒谎时，他总会找一个合理的、高尚的理由，也会说是为了别人。

One day, while a woodcutter was cutting a branch of a tree above a river, his axe[1] fell into the river. When he cried out, the Lord appeared and asked, "Why are you crying?"

The woodcutter replied that his axe has <u>fallen into</u>[2] the water, and he needed the axe to make his living.

The Lord went down into the water and reappeared with a golden axe. "Is this your axe?" the Lord asked.

The woodcutter replied, "No." The Lord again went down and <u>came up</u>[3] with a silver axe. "Is this your axe?" the Lord asked.

Again, the woodcutter replied, "No."

The Lord went down again and came up with an iron axe. "Is this your axe?" the Lord asked.

The woodcutter replied, "Yes."

The Lord was pleased with the man's honesty and gave him all three axes to keep, and the woodcutter went home happily.

Some time later the woodcutter was walking with his wife along the riverbank, and his wife fell into the river. When he cried out, the Lord again appeared and asked him, "Why are you crying?"

一天，一个樵夫在河边砍树枝时，他的斧头掉进河里了，他大声哭起来。上帝出现了，问他："你为什么哭啊？"

樵夫回答说他的斧头掉进河里了，他还要用斧头谋生呢。

上帝钻进了水里，出来时手里拿了一把金斧头。"这是你的斧头吗？"上帝问。

樵夫说："不是。"上帝又钻进了水里，出来时手里拿了一把银斧头。"这是你的斧头吗？"上帝问。

樵夫又说："不是。"

上帝又下去，拿了一把铁斧头出来。"这是你的斧头吗？"上帝问。

樵夫回答说："是的。"

上帝很高兴这个人很诚实，把三把斧头都给了他。樵夫很高兴地回家了。

后来，樵夫和妻子在河边散步时，妻子掉进河里了。他大哭，上帝又出现了问他："你为什么哭啊？"

"上帝啊，我的妻子掉进河里了！"

上帝钻进水里，和詹妮弗·洛佩兹一起出来了。

"这是你的妻子吗？"上帝问。

"是的。" 樵夫叫道。

上帝大发雷霆，"你撒谎，这根本不是

❶ axe /æks/
n. 斧头
❷ fell into
掉进
❸ come up
出现

"Oh Lord, my wife has fallen into the water!"

The Lord went down into the water and came up with Jennifer Lopez.

"Is this your wife?" the Lord asked.

"Yes," cried the woodcutter.

The Lord was furious[4], "You lied! That is an untruth!"

The woodcutter replied, "Oh, forgive me, my Lord, it is a misunderstanding[5].

"You see, if I had said 'no' to Jennifer Lopez, you would have come up with Catherine Zeta-Jones. Then if I also said 'no' to her, you would have come up with my wife. Had I then said 'yes,' you would have given all three to me.

"Lord, I am a poor man, and am not able to take care of all three wives, so THAT'S why I said yes to Jennifer Lopez."

The moral of this story is: Whenever a man lies, it is for a good and honorable reason, and for the benefit of others.

That's our story, and we're <u>sticking to</u>[6] it.

真的!"

樵夫回答道:"上帝,原谅我吧,这是个误会。"

"你看,如果我说不是詹妮弗·洛佩兹,你可能会带凯瑟琳·泽塔—琼斯出来。我如果还说不是她,你又会带我的妻子出来。如果我那时说"是",你就会把她们三人都给我。上帝啊,我很穷,养活不了三个妻子,这就是我为什么说是詹妮弗·洛佩兹的原因。"

这个故事的寓意是:当一个人撒谎时,他总会找一个合理的、高尚的理由,也会说是为了别人。

这就是我们的经历,我们也一直在这样做。

❹ furious
/ˈfjʊərɪəs/
adj. 狂怒的,暴怒的
❺ misunderstanding
/ˌmɪsʌndəˈstændɪŋ/
n. 误会
❻ stick to
紧跟,紧随

Money and love,
which one you will choose?

金钱和爱情
你会怎样选择

You don't want to apart with him or her, while the real life urges you to choose another life.

你不想和他或她分开，但现实生活迫使你选择另一种生活。

I think I will choose money. Though every girl dreams roman-tic love, meets a handsome boy, and falls in love with[1] him. But this is only an ideality[2], you can choose love before marriage, you can treat it as snack[3], just to enrich your life. But real society is very true; you should take everything into consideration. When you get married, you will have to settled your love cabin[4], which will cost a lot of money, you will form a abroad relationship, which you and your lover have to face, once you have children, you will be worried about their education fund, what I mentioned all needs money.

But if you get married with a poor man, maybe you will be happy at the beginning of the marriage, because of spirit wealth, and the money you both earn is just enough for basic life. But several months or several years later, you will quarrel for money, then your life run into affliction[5]. You feel contradiction[6], one is your lover you love him or her very much, one is the real life you have to face. You don't want to apart with him or her, while the real life urges you to choose another life. Face such situation, you will suffer feeling agonies[7].

But once you get married with a rich man who you love not so deeply, maybe you will get material wealth, and enjoy this happy from money. And when you divorce, you will not feel so sad in your feeling.

　　我想我会选择金钱。尽管每个女孩都梦想有浪漫的爱情，希望遇到一个英俊的男孩，和他恋爱，但是这只是一个理想。结婚前你可以选择爱情，把它当作甜点，这样你的生活会变得丰富多彩。但是真实的社会很现实，你必须全方位考虑。结婚时你必须要建筑爱巢，这需要一大笔钱，你和你的爱人会有必须面对的广泛的关系网，一旦你有了孩子，你还要担心他的教育花费。我所提到的这些都需要钱。

　　但是如果你和一个穷人结婚，可能婚姻开始时幸福，因为你们有精神财富，两个人挣的钱也能满足基本生活需要。但是几个月、几年后，你们就会为钱而争吵，你们的生活就要陷入痛苦之中。你会很矛盾，一边是你的爱人，你非常爱他或她，一边是现实生活，你必须面对。你不想和他或她分开，但现实生活迫使你选择另一种生活。在这种情况下，你一定会陷入极度痛苦之中。

　　但是一旦你和一个富人结婚，尽管你不太爱他，但是你会得到物质财富，也会享受有钱的幸福。当你离婚时，你也不会感到特别伤心。

❶ fall in love with
爱上
❷ ideality
/ˌaɪdɪˈælətɪ/
n. 理想的事物
❸ snack
/snæk/
n. 甜点
❹ love cabin
爱巢
❺ affliction
/əˈflɪkʃən/
n. 苦恼的事
❻ contradiction
/ˌkɒntrəˈdɪkʃən/
n. 矛盾
❼ agony
/ˈæɡənɪ/
n. (极度的)痛苦

Life style: ant or butterfly

生活方式:蚂蚁和蝴蝶

In a man's youth, you can choose your own life style and you will pay for it after you are getting old but you won't know because you are too young.

在青年时期,你可以选择你自己的生活方式,但等你老了,一定会为此付出代价,但是你太年轻,还不知道这些。

Recently I have read a piece of *Aesop's Fables*. As you know that Aesop was very good at using animals and insects[1] to express the truth of life. In that story, butterfly felt hungry in winter so it went to ant for food and help. Ant asked butterfly a question: "What do you do in summer?" "I was dancing in the whole summer." Butterfly uttered[2]. Ant smiled and said, "You can sing in winter if you like."

It is a really short story with deep thoughts. Four seasons can symbolize[3] the life of a man. Spring is the childhood and summer could be youth. Fall is middle age and winter must be old age.

You can choose your life in an ant's way or a butterfly's way. To be an ant, you are working hard for years with tame[4]. In the anthill, you know that you are a part of it and you must work hard as others. The target is very clear—everything you do is to build the anthill for survival and better life. As a butterfly, you are dancing among the flowers elegantly. You choose what you like and you run away if you hate or feel uncomfortable. Satisfaction to yourself is the basic stand of your life. You are very happy and beautiful. Even you think that life will keep steady[5] for you and your talents.

In a man's youth, you can choose your own life style and you will pay for it after you are getting old but you won't know because you are too young. You are very brave to do a lot and accept everything. You are also too quick to make the decision for the benefits in your eyes range.

It is really touched me. For the work, I never think that I try

最近我读到一则《伊索寓言》。我们都知道伊索非常擅长用动物和昆虫来表达生活的真谛。那个故事写的是蝴蝶在冬天很饿，于是它去找蚂蚁寻求食物和帮助。蚂蚁问蝴蝶："你夏天都干嘛了？""我整个夏天都在跳舞。"蝴蝶说。蚂蚁笑着说："那么在冬天你可以唱歌啊！"

这个故事虽短却含义深刻。四个季节可以象征人的一生：春天代表童年，夏天代表青年，秋天代表中年，冬天代表老年。

你可以选择蚂蚁的生活方式，也可以选择蝴蝶的生活方式。作为蚂蚁你要成年任劳任愿地努力工作，你知道你只是蚁山的一个成员，必须像其他人一样努力工作，目标很明确——你做的每一件事都是为了蚁山的生存并为之创造更幸福的生活。作为一只蝴蝶，你在花丛中优雅地跳舞。你选择你喜欢的，如果你不喜欢或感到不舒服，你可以跑得远远的。使自己满意是选择生活方式最基本的标准。你很幸福、很美丽，甚至认为因为你和你的才能，生活会一路平坦。

在青年时期，你可以选择你自己的生活方式，但等你老了，一定会为此付出代价，但是你太年轻，还不知道这些。你很勇敢，做了很多事情，什么都接受。你也会为了眼前的利益而做出仓促的决定。

我真的为之触动了。对于工作，我从来

❶ insect
/ˈɪnsekt/
n. 昆虫
❷ utter /ˈʌtə(r)/
v. 说
❸ symbolize
/ˈsɪmbəlaɪz/
v. 象征
❹ tame /teɪm/
v. 驯服
❺ steady
/ˈstedɪ/
adj. 平稳的

my best. For my family, I never contribute enough. I am so inconstant[6] to jump between an ant and a butterfly. I have planned many things for my life but few are realized by my patience and efforts. As a matter of fact, my plan is not really impossible to access[7]. It failed because of my laze[8] and hesitation. From today, I will try to achieve my success little by little.

没想过尽力去做；对于家庭，我也没有付出太多。我总是反复在蚂蚁和蝴蝶之间徘徊。我为我的生活制定了很多计划，但是没有几个计划我付出了耐心和努力。事实上，我的计划也不是真正不可以实现，没有实现是由于我的懒散和犹豫。从今天开始，我要尽力一点一点争取成功。

❻ inconstant
/ɪnˈkɒnstənt/
adj. 反复无常的
❼ access
/ˈækses/
v. 接近
❽ laze
/leɪz/
n. 懒散

Adventure in San Francisco

旧金山历险记

When I was out of the smoky, rocky place, I felt so dizzy and sleepy but was glad that I was safe and sound.

当我走出烟雾弥漫、嘈杂混乱的地方时，我感到头昏、疲倦，但是还是很高兴我安然无恙。

So far the most dramatic day in my life was spent in San Francisco. The whole day that day, starting from 6 am to 9 pm I was in casinos[1] in Reno. Almost in the middle of nowhere, Reno's economy was sustained by its gambling industry.

The fist casino I went to was called "Feather Falls Casino". Surprisingly almost 80% of the gamblers were senior citizens. Old and feeble[2] as they may usually be, these people definitely presented a more energetic side of their life. I soon realized I'm not a casino girl just after ten minutes' trying. For one thing, I thought the games were pretty boring. For another, I standed little chance to win. And if you're not rewarded for what you are doing for long, you'll get bored soon. After losing twenty-five bucks, I stopped trying my luck. It seldom stroke me and never in a casino.

After three hours drive I was back in the place where we were staying. It was almost 9 pm, but within an hour and half, I was out again with my traveling mate Lazaro and his friends who invited me to a nightclub. I had no idea of what a nightclub was like. Simply out of curiosity I followed them.

The moment I stepped in that property, I knew something weird was going on. It was a two-storied building, dimly lit, litters around. We paid eighteen dollars each for admission (That's quite expensive, isn't it?) and three more dollars for checking in our jackets (This is outrageous!). What were all these bucks for? There must be something special about this place.

1 casino
/kəˈsiːnəʊ/
n. 赌场

2 feeble
/ˈfiːbl/
adj. 衰弱的

到现在为止，我生命中最富戏剧性的一天是在旧金山度过的。那一整天从早上6点到晚上9点，我都在里诺的赌场。里诺位于美国中部，没有其他产业，它的经济是靠其赌博业支撑的。

我去的第一家赌场叫"羽毛飘落"赌场。奇怪的是，那里80%的赌徒都是老年人。尽管他们平时都年老体衰，但是，在这里，他们都无疑表现出生命中更加精力充沛的一面。仅仅在这儿玩了10分钟，我马上意识到我还不是一个赌场女孩。一方面我觉得赌博很无聊，另一方面我几乎没有机会赢。如果你玩了很长时间还不赢的话，你会很快感到厌烦的。输了25美元之后我不想碰运气了。我很少有好运气，在赌场里更是从来都没有过。

开车行驶了3小时后我回到了原来的地方，那时已经是晚上9点了。但是一个半小时后，我又出去了，因为我的旅行同伴Lazaro和他的朋友们邀请我去一家夜总会。我不知道夜总会是什么样，只是出于好奇我才跟他们去了。

在踏进这家夜总会的那一刻，我就感觉到有什么怪异的事情在发生。这是一幢两层楼，灯光很暗，到处都是纸屑。我们花了18

I followed my friends down the dark hallway and then into a crowded room. Loud music was rocking down the roof. Gosh! On several tables scattered around the room, there were people dancing nastily! I guessed you would call them male strippers[3].

"What the heck is that!" (Forgive me for the language.)

I looked at my friends. They were definitely engrossed in[4] the scene. Their faces were lit up[5], with sparks of excitement in their eyes. And, Lazaro's two friends were holding hands now. Lazaro himself also looked a little different. I may be a dumb girl in many ways, but by now I had figured out what was going on. Gee, I was in a gay club with three gay guys! But I was straight. Tonight was doomed to be quite an unforgettable experience.

All right. Take it easy, baby! I told myself. Let's see what's going to happen.

They bought me a drink. One of the advantages of being a girl is that there are always gentlemen (gentle ladies in this case?) who'll take care of your bill.

Taking a sip of the drink, I tried to calm down. Dances were still going on. The atmosphere was spiced up[6]. People were scream-ing. I forgot to mention that most of the people there were gay guys. I only saw several girls, one of whom looked definitely way too femin ine. I could not repress[7] my curiosity, so I turned to Lazaro and asked him what was wrong with that "girl".

美元买门票（很贵，是不是?），还为检查夹克衫花了 3 美元（真是欺人太甚!）。为什么要花这些钱呢？这个地方一定有问题。

我随朋友们顺着黑暗的走廊进了一间拥挤的房间，音乐响得快把屋顶震塌了，几张桌子凌乱地放在屋子里，有几个人在很恶心地跳舞。我猜想你会觉得他们是男脱衣舞表演者。

"这是他妈的什么呀!"（原谅我这样说。）

我看着我的朋友们，他们都已经全身心投入到这个场合中了，脸上容光焕发，眼里闪烁着兴奋，而且 Lazaro 的两个朋友现在还牵起手来。Lazaro 看起来也有些异常。我可能在很多方面都是一个迟钝的女孩，直到现在我才明白发生了什么。天哪! 我和 3 个同性恋在一家同性恋俱乐部里! 但是我很正直，今晚注定是一次很难忘记的经历。

算了，放松点! 我告诉自己，看看会发生什么。

他们给我买了一瓶饮料。作为女孩子的一个好处就是经常会有男士（这种情况下应该是男女士）为你付账。

我喝了一小口饮料，尽力平静下来。他们还在跳舞，气氛很刺激，人们在尖叫。我

❸ **stripper**
/'strɪpə(r)/
n. 脱衣舞表演者
❹ **be engrossed in**
全神贯注
❺ **light up**
容光焕发
❻ **spice up**
刺激
❼ **repress**
/rɪ'pres/
v. 压制，抑制

"A drag queen," Lazaro surely knew more than I do.

When "she" passed me by, my eyes followed "her" till "she" was out of my sight. I was being very impolite, but who cared here? Ho, ho, curiosity may kill the cat, but not me.

My friends were having a very good time, but I got bored pretty soon. There was no common ground between us anyway. Worse still, I felt like going to the restroom. So I looked around and found the spot. But when I was about to enter the room with the sign "Ladies" on the door, I heard men talking inside. I withdrew my step in total confusion. Was I at the wrong door? I looked up. I was right. Then what were those guys doing there?

Out of shock, I returned to my friends. "Well, that's because they think they are ladies and of course they have the right to use ladies' room!" I was told so. But what was I gonna do then?

I didn't want to be a wet blanket[8] and say I'm leaving. Besides, I didn't drive so I couldn't get back by myself. So I decided I would just hold it and wait till they were ready to leave. Had I known that it would be a three-hour waiting, I would have made a better decision.

I was beginning to feel uneasy standing in the corner, trying to get a little far away from the commotion[9] when an Asian girl coming up to me. " Do you know where I can get ecstasy[10]?" she asked me.

忘记说了，那里的很多人都是同性恋。我只看到几个女孩，其中一个人看起来太女性化了。我抑制不住好奇心，于是我转向 Lazaro 问他那个"女孩"怎么了。

"他是男扮女装的王后。" Lazaro 显然比我知道的多。

当"她"经过我身旁时，我一直盯着"她"看，直到"她"从我的视线中消失。我很不礼貌，但谁会在意呢？呵呵，好奇心可能会杀死一只猫，但不会杀死我。

我的朋友们玩得很高兴，但我很快就厌烦了。我们之间没有共同兴趣，更糟的是我想去卫生间。我看了看四周，找到了地方，但是，正当我要走进门上写着"女"的卫生间时，我听到里面有男人在说话。我完全糊涂了，缩回了脚。我走错了吗？我抬头看了看，没错。那么那些男人在那做什么呢？

我大吃一惊，回到朋友那儿。"哦，那是因为他们认为他们是女士，当然有权力使用女厕所了！"他们告诉我。但我怎么办呢？

我不想当一个扫兴的人，说我要离开，而且我不会开车，所以我自己回不去。于是我决定忍受一下，等一等，和他们一起回去。如果我早知道要等 3 个小时，我就会做一个更好的决定。

⑧ a wet blanket
扫兴的人
⑨ commotion
/kə'məʊʃən/
n. 混乱
⑩ ecstasy
n. 狂喜；"灵魂出窍"迷幻药

"What?" I could not make head or tail of her question.

"Ecstasy?" the girl repeated the word.

Still having no clue of what this meant, I gave her a puzzled look.

"Never mind", she shrugged and left.

"Somebody just asked me about ecstasy. What's that?" I turned to my friends for help again, feeling sorry for being so ignorant.

"Aha, she thought you were part of their group. Ecstasy is a drug popular among Asians."

"Jesus!" I exclaimed.

It took me quite some time to get over the shock from the drug episode[11]. I took a few more sips of the drink to gather myself although by then the thought of going to the restroom was heavy on my mind.

I waited and waited till three o'clock in the morning. When I was out of the smoky, rocky place, I felt so dizzy and sleepy but was glad that I was safe and sound[12].

站在角落里我开始感到不自在，想要远离这混乱的场面，这时一个亚洲女孩走近我问："你知道哪儿有狂喜粉吗?"

"什么?"我没听明白她的问题。

"狂喜粉。"女孩重复了一遍。

我还是不明白她指的是什么，显得很迷惑。

"没关系。"她耸了耸肩，离开了。

"有人刚才问我狂喜粉，那是什么?"我又向朋友求助，对我的无知感到很不好意思。

"啊，她以为你也吸毒呢。狂喜粉是亚洲流行的一种毒品。"

"上帝!"我惊叫道。

我花了好长时间才从毒品插曲中回过神来。我喝了几口饮料使自己镇静，尽管那时我特别想上厕所。

我等啊等，一直等到凌晨3点钟。当我走出烟雾弥漫、嘈杂混乱的地方时，我感到头昏、疲倦，但是还是很高兴我很安然无恙。

⓫ episode
/ˈepɪsəʊd/
n. 插曲，片段
⓬ sound /saʊd/
adj. 完好的，无损伤的

I am going to put you in jail

我要把你们送进监狱

Suddenly, she noticed that some police car was behind her, and the lights on the car were flashing.

突然我的室友注意到有一辆警车跟在她后面,车上的警灯还在闪烁。

This story is about my first roommate in the States.

The story happened even before she got her Driver's license[1].

That was our first semester in the States. We shared a one-bedroom on campus. There were on campus shuttles[2] to all the main buildings, so school was not a problem for us. As both of us were new to the States and none of us had a car, shopping was the biggest problem for us. We had to car pool with someone who did have a car. So we could only go shopping once a week or twice a month.

That was so inconvenient[3], so my roommate decided to buy a car ASAP. And she bought a car after about 2 months. She was the first one of us new students to have a car! She got a learner's permit right away, so she started her first driving experience.

There was a river near where we live, and the bridge on it was the shortest path for shopping. She decided to practice her driving on road instead of the parking lot. So she went shopping with someone who had almost half year of driving experience sitting on the passenger seat.(I shall call him L). That (someone with a driver's license) was required to be in the car when you only had a learner's permit. On their way back, she was supposed to be at the left turn lane[4], but she lined up[5] in the go straightforward lane . So my roommate asked L—

Roommate: "Hi, L, Can I make a left turn on this lane or should

这个故事说的是我在美国第一个室友的经历。

这件事发生在她拿到驾照之前。

那是我们在美国的第一学期，我们住在校园里的同一间宿舍里，有校车通往各个主楼，所以对我们来说上学不成问题。因为我们都是初来美国，都没有车，购物成了我们最大的问题。我们只有和有车的人一起去，所以我们只能一个星期购一次物或两个星期一次。

这真不方便，所以我的室友决定要尽快买一辆车，大约两个月后她买了一辆。她是我们这些新生中最先买车的！她立即获得了新手上路的资格，于是她开始了第一次驾车经历。

我们宿舍附近有一条河，过桥是去购物最近的路。她决定在路上练习开车，而不在停车场练习。于是她开车去购物，副驾驶座上坐的是大约有半年驾龄的同伴（我叫他L）。按要求，新手上路车上必须要坐一个已拿驾照的人。回来的时候，她本应该行驶在左转的车道上，但她却排在直行的车道上了。于是，我的室友问L——

室友："L，我在这条道上可以左转吗？还是我应该直行，绕一大圈后再回来？"

❶ driver's license
驾照
❷ campus shuttle
校车
❸ inconvenient
/ˌɪnkən'viːnjənt/
adj.不方便的
❹ lane /leɪn/
n.车道
❺ line up
n. 排列起

I go straight forward and U turn back?"

L: "It's OK to turn, just keep going!"

So my roommate listened to him, though with a little doubt

Suddenly, she noticed that some police car was behind her, and the lights on the car were flashing. She was a little scared[6], so —

Roommate: "Hi, L, did you see the police behind? Is he following us? Do I need to stop?"

L: "I don't think so. We didn't do anything wrong, why us? Just keep going."

Roommate: "Are you sure? The police car is still following us with siren[7] on and lights flashing!" Though she was still asking, she didn't stop as she <u>was very concentrated on</u>[8] her driving.

Before they could think of any reason why the cops were after them, they heard huge siren!

Before she had any single idea, several police cars stopped them!

One front, two beside, two behind!

L："可以转弯，开吧！"

于是我的室友尽管有一些疑惑，还是听了他的话。

突然我的室友注意到有一辆警车跟在她后面，车上的警灯还在闪烁。她有点害怕，所以——

室友问："L，你看见后面的警车了吗？是不是在追我们？我需要停下来吗？"

L："不用，我们又没做错什么，为什么要停下来？继续开吧！"

室友："你确定吗？警车在追赶我们，警笛在响，警灯在闪呢！"尽管她一直在问，但还是没停下来，她开得太专注了。

他们还没想出任何警察要追他们的理由，就听到了震耳的警笛声。

她还来不及有任何想法，几辆警车就拦住了他们。

前面一辆，旁边两辆，后面两辆！

她很惊慌，不知道出了什么事。她决定下车问警察。她刚打开门，一个警察就拿着枪对着她大声说道："不许动！"

哦，天哪！这是一次什么经历！她说那时她害怕得要死。警察让她把双手放在脑袋上！而且L也同样被要求这样做。

另一个警察跑过来问她："为什么不停

❻ scared /skeəd/ *adj.* 恐惧的
❼ siren /ˈsaɪərɪn/ *n.* 警笛
❽ be concentrated on 聚精会神

She was so scared and didn't know what was wrong. She decided to get off and ask the police. At the moment she opened her door, one cop came up with a gun pointing to her and shouted, "Freeze!"

Oh, Gosh! What an experience! She said she was scared to death at that moment. She was then told to put both hands on her head! And L was told to do the same thing!

Another cop ran up and asked her: "Why didn't you stop? Don't you know that you need to pull to the roadside and come to a full stop when you see our lights flashing? I AM GOING TO PUT YOU IN JAIL!"

Oh, MY GOODNESS! My roommate was so scared that she started to weep: "I ... d ... di ... did didn't ... know ..." The cops checked their driver's license and registration[9], when they knew that she was just learning to drive, they began to shout at L! Luckily, there was one Asian cop, he was really nice, and he said something to the other cops and let them go at last.

车？你难道不知道看到我们的警灯闪烁时应该靠路边停下来吗？我要把你们送进监狱！"

上帝！我的室友害怕得开始哭了。"我…我…不…不…知道…"警察看了看他们的的驾照和证件，当他们知道她只是初次开车上路时，他们对 L 大声呵斥起来。幸运的是有一个亚洲警察，人很好，他对其他警察说了几句话，最后让他们走了。

9 registration
/ˌredʒɪˈstreɪʃən/
n. 登记

I knew these people

我认识这些人

For the first time, he wished to went far away, lost in a deep, vast country where nobody knew him. Somewhere without language, or streets.

第一次，他想跑到很遥远的地方，消失在一个没有人认识他的广袤无垠的国家里。那里没有语言，也没有街道。

I knew these people narrated[1] by Harry Dean Stanton and Nastassja Kinski.

I knew these people. These two people...(coughing)...They were in love with each other.

The girl was very young, about 17 or 18 I guess. And the guy was quite a bit older. He was kind of ragged and wild. And she was very beautiful, you know. And together they turned everything into a kind of adventure. And she liked that. Just going a trip down to the grocery store was full of adventure. They were always laughing at stupid things. He liked to make her laugh. And they didn't much care for anything else because all they wanted to do was to be with each other. They were always together. And he loved her more than he ever felt possible.

He couldn't stand being away from her during the day when he went to work. So he quit, just to be home with her. Then he get another job when the money ran out[2], then he quit again. But pretty soon she started to worry. (Like what?) Money I guess. Not having enough. Not knowing when the next check was coming in. (Yap, I know that feeling.) So he started to get kind of torn inside. (How do you mean?) Well, he knew he had to work support her, but he couldn't stand being away from her, either. (I see.) And the more he was away from her, the crazier he got. Except now, he got really crazy.

He started to imagine in all kinds of things.(Like what?) He started to think that she was seeing another man on the slide[3]. He

　　我认识 Harry Dean Stanton 和 Nastassja Kinski 所讲述的这些人。

　　我认识这些人。这两个人 …… （清清嗓子）……他们正在谈爱。

　　女孩很年轻，我猜大约十七八岁。小伙子比她大一点。他穿着破旧的衣服，很粗野，她却很漂亮。他俩一起把一切都变成了一种冒险活动。她喜欢那样，就算是去杂货店买东西也充满冒险。他们总是嘲笑愚蠢的事情。他喜欢逗她大笑，他们不在乎其他任何事情，他们想做的就是彼此在一起，他们总是在一起。他不顾一切地爱她。

　　当去上班时他不能忍受离开她，于是他辞掉了工作，仅仅是为了在家陪她。没钱花的时候，他又找了一份工作，后来又辞了。但是不久她开始担心（担心什么呢?），我猜是担心钱不够花，不知道何时会有下一笔收入。（咳，我知道那种感觉），所以他的内心开始撕扯（什么意思呢?）。他知道他必须工作养活她，但又不能忍受离开她（我明白了）。他离开她的时间越长，他就变得越疯狂。现在他是不能了，但当时他真的变得很疯狂了。

　　他开始想像各种事情（什么呢?）。他开始想像他看到她和另一个男人在滑道上。他

① **narrate**
/nəˈreɪt/
v. 讲述；描述

② **run out**
用完，耗尽

③ **slide** /slaɪd/
n. 滑道

came home from work and accused her spending the day with somebody else. He yelled[4] at her and broke things on the trailer[5]. (The trailer?) Yes, they lived in a trailer home. Anyway, he started to drink really bad and he stayed out late to test her, to see if she got jealous. He wanted her to get jealous. But she didn't. She just worried about him. That got him even madder. He thought that she never got jealous meant that she never really cared about him. Jealousy was a sign of her love for him.

And then one night, she told him that she was pregnant. She was about 3 or 4 months pregnant. And he didn't even know. And then suddenly everything changed. He stopped drinking. He got a steady job. He was convinced that she loved him now because she was carrying his child. And he was going to dedicate himself to making a home for her. But the funny thing started to happen. He didn't even notice it at first. She started to change. The day the baby was born, she began to get irritated[6] at everything around her. She got mad at everything. Even the baby seems to be an injustice to her. He kept on doing everything all right for her. Buy her things. Take her out for dinner once a week. But nothing seemed to satisfy her.

For 2 years, he struggled to pull them back together like they were when they first met. But finally he knew that it was never gonna work out. So he hit the bottle[7] again. But this time he got mean. This time when he came home late at night, she wasn't worried about him or jealous. She was just enraged[8]. She accused him of holding her a captive[9] by having her have a baby. She told him that she dreamed about escaping. That was all

工作后回到家，骂她和别人呆了一天。他冲她大吼大叫，还摔活动房屋里的东西。（活动房屋？）是的，他们住在活动房屋里。不管怎样，他开始喝得酩酊大醉，在外面呆到很晚，以此来考验她，看她是否会嫉妒。他希望她嫉妒，但她没有，她只是担心他。这使他疯得更厉害了。他认为她不嫉妒就意味着她从没有真正在乎他。嫉妒表示她爱他。

一天晚上，她告诉他怀孕有3、4个月了，他竟然一点都不知道。突然一切都改变了。他戒了酒，找了一份稳定的工作。他现在相信她是爱他的，因为她怀了他的孩子。他决定全力为她营造一个家。但是滑稽的事情发生了，他甚至最初都没注意到：她开始变了。孩子出生的当天，她就开始厌烦她周围的一切。她看什么都来气，甚至觉得小孩对她来说也是不公平的。他还是继续做使她高兴的事情，给她买东西，每周带她出去吃一次饭，但还是没有任何事情使她满意。

两年来，他一直想让他们找回第一次见面时的感觉，但是最后他知道这根本不可能，所以他又经常酗酒。这一次他变得很堕落，很晚回家，而她不担心他，也不嫉妒他，只是恼怒。她指责他让她生小孩只是想拴住她。她告诉他，她做梦都想逃离，她所

④ **yell** /jel/
v. 大声叫嚷
⑤ **trailer**
/'treɪlə(r)/
n. 汽车拖的活动住房
⑥ **irritated**
/'ɪrɪteɪtɪd/
adj. 烦恼的
⑦ **hit the bottle**
酗酒
⑧ **enraged**
/ɪn'reɪdʒɪd/
adj. 愤怒的
⑨ **captive**
/'kæptɪv/
adj. 被俘的

she dreamed about: escape. She saw herself at night, running naked down the highway, running across fields, running down riverbeds, always running. And always just when she was about to get away, he'd be there. He would stop her somehow. He would just appear and stop her.

And when she told him these dreams. He believed them. He knew she had to be stopped, or she'd leave him forever. So he tied a cowbell to her ankle. So he could hear her at night if she tried to get out of the bed. But she learned to muffle[10] the bell by stuffing a stocking into it and inching[11] away, out of the bed, and into the night. He caught her one night when the sock fell out and he heard her trying to run to the highway. He caught her, and dragged her back to the trailer, and tied her to the stove with his belt. He just left her there, went back to bed and laid there listening to her scream. And he listened to his son scream. He was surprised at himself because he didn't feel anything anymore. All he wanted to do was sleep.

For the first time, he wished to went far away, lost in a deep, vast country where nobody knew him. Somewhere without language, or streets. And he dreamed about this place without knowing its name. And when he woke up, he was on fire. There were blue flames burning the sheets of his bed. He ran through the flames, for the only 2 people he loved. But they were gone. His arms were burning. And he threw himself outside and rolled on the wet ground. And he ran. He never looked back at the fire. He just ran.

有的梦想就是：逃离。她看见她自己晚上光着身子在高速公路上跑，穿过田野，越过河床，一直跑。总是在她正要离开时，他出现了，而且会想办法阻止她。他一定会及时出现阻拦她的。

当她把这些梦告诉他时，他相信了。他知道一定要阻拦她，否则她一定会永远地离开他，所以他在她脚踝上系了一个牛颈铃，这样当她晚上想下床时，他就可以听见。但是，她知道往里面塞袜子铃就不响了，然后下床慢慢地走向黑夜。有一天晚上他抓住了她，因为铃里的袜子掉了出来，他听到她企图跑向高速公路的声音。他抓住她，把她拽回活动房屋，用他的皮带把她绑在炉子上。他把她扔在那儿，自己回到床上，躺在那儿听她尖叫。然后他又听见儿子的哭喊声。他很惊讶自己居然对这一切竟无动于衷。他只是想睡觉。

第一次，他想跑到很遥远的地方，消失在一个没有人认识他的广袤无垠的国家里。那里没有语言，也没有街道。他梦见了这个他不知道名字的地方。当他醒来时，身上着火了。蓝色的火焰正在燃烧他的床单。他冲出火焰去救他最爱的两个人，但是他们不见了。他的胳膊也烧起来了，他跑出去，在湿地上打起滚来，接着跑了起来，再也没回头

⑩ muffle /'mʌfl/
v. 包住
⑪ inch /ɪntʃ/
v. 慢慢移动

He ran until the sun came up and he couldn't run any further. And when the sun went down, he ran again. For five days he ran like this, until every sign of the man had disappeared.

看一眼正在燃烧的火焰，只是跑。

　　他一直跑到太阳升起来，再也跑不动了。
当太阳落山时，他又跑起来。他像这样一连
跑了5天，直到最后停止了呼吸。

A lesson for life
生活的启示

Simple and sincere gestures sometimes can have far reaching effects on them and life may never be the same again.

简单真诚的手势有时会给他们深远的影响，从此他们的生活便会不同。

One morning Sanggat, an eight-year-old pupil of mine, knocked on my door; he was here to help me sweep my quarters[1]. He noticed some thick books neatly arranged on my reading table.

Curiously he asked, "Sir, what books are these?" I told him that those were books that I needed to study for an important exam so that I might go to university someday. He frowned[2] because in a remote area where we were, even a bicycle was unheard of. I tried to explain university to him with the help of pictures that looked like a university campus. At that time, Sarawak did not have a university and the nearest one was across the South China Sea, in Peninsular Malaysia.

He was surprised, "But, sir, you are a teacher. Why study?"

So we sat down and I told him all about this thing called Education and gave him a pep talk[3] about his chances of becoming someone great in the future. He took one of my books the thickest one in his hands and upon opening it exclaimed[4], "Now, the words are so tiny and there are millions of them. How can you possibly finish reading it?"

I explained to him the importance of learning to read well and to make the best out of the lessons that he was learning at school, and that teachers like me, were specially sent to teach special children like him so that someday they could read great books like the one he was holding. He left my room.

When the other pupils learned that Sanggat always volunteered

一天早上，我的一个学生——8岁的Sanggat敲响了我的门，他是来帮我打扫房间的。他注意到有几本厚厚的书整齐地摆在我的书桌上。

他很好奇地问我："这些是什么书？"我告诉他这些书是我参加重要的大学入学考试需要看的。他听完之后，皱起了眉头，因为在我们这样一个偏远的地方，连自行车都没有听说过。我借助几张看起来像是大学校园的照片给他解释大学是什么样的。那时沙捞越州还没有大学，最近的一所是在穿过中国南海的马来西亚半岛。

他很吃惊地问道："但是先生，你是老师，怎么还要学习？"

我们坐下来，我给他讲有关教育的事情，鼓励他将来有机会成为伟大的人。他拿起最厚的一本书，打开一看，惊叫道："字这么小，有几百万呢，你怎么看得完呢？"

我告诉他，学会读书并且领悟在校所学课程的精华是很重要的，而且像我这样的老师就是特地派来教像他这样的特殊学生的，将来有一天，他们也能读像他手上拿的一些大部头的书。他离开了我的房间。

① quarter

/ˈkwɔːtə(r)/

n. 住处

② frown /fraʊn/

v. 皱眉

③ pep talk

鼓励的话

④ exclaim

/ɪksˈkleɪm/

v. 惊叫

to sweep my room, they wanted to do the same and soon it became an almost daily ritual[5] which ended up with me buying more
brooms to maximize[6] participation. And Sanggat would never fail
to show them my books, each time adding a little commentary of
his own about them in the Iban language.

I did not realize the impact my words had on him until the day
I slipped into the river and broke my neck. I was to be paralyzed[7]
from my shoulders downward for the rest of my life.

I was carried into a speedboat and transported back to
civilization. As I lay motionless and exhausted, I noticed that the
whole school had gathered by the riverside to bid me farewell. A
gaze at their faces told me that I was going to miss them. Then,
as the engine of the speedboat started to roar, there was a little
commotion by the river.

I could see Sanggat making his way to the boat. With tear-filled
eyes he approached and in between sobs he asked, "Sir, are you
coming back? Perhaps not?"

Then after a short pause he said, "Sir, if you cannot come
back, I'll see you in the university, ya?"

My heart was profoundly touched and as the boat moved
away, I realized an important lesson of my own: Teachers must never
fail to take time explaining positive lessons to the young ones.
Simple and sincere gestures sometimes can have far reaching

其他学生知道Sangga经常自愿来帮我打扫房间后，他们也想这样做。于是不久，这几乎成了每天例行的仪式，最后我只有多买些扫帚，使更多的人参与进来。Sanggat总是把我的书拿给他们看，每次都用伊巴语发表一下自己的见解。

我从来没有意识到我的话对他有什么影响，直到有一天我滑进河里，摔断了脖子，肩部以下终生瘫痪。

我被抬进快艇返回城市。当我躺在那儿一动不动、全身疲倦的时候，我注意到全校的学生都聚集到河边来和我道别。看着他们的脸，我就知道我会想念他们的。当快艇的发动机响起来时，河边有一阵小小的骚动。

我看到Sanggat向船走过来，眼里含着泪水。他抽噎着问我："老师，您还回来吗？还是不回来了？"

过了一会儿他说："老师，如果您不能回来，我们在大学里相见，好吗？"

我的心被深深的触动了。当船离开时，我自己意识到一个重要的启示：老师必须不忘给学生积极的教育。简单真诚的手势有时会对他们产生深远的影响，他们的生活也会

❺ ritual /ˈrɪtjʊəl/
n. 仪式
❻ maximize
/ˈmæksmaɪz/
v. 使增至最大限度
❼ paralyze
/ˈpærəlaɪz/
v. 瘫痪

effects on them and life may never be the same again. It is the small simple pleasures we gather from life that ultimately bear great fruits of profound magnitude[8]. We should watch out for every opportunity we have to assist the young ones towards self-accomplishments.

因此而改变。正是我们从生活中得到的点滴的快乐最终结出了丰硕的果实。我们必须抓住每一个机会来帮助年轻人实现自我价值。

❽ magnitude
/ˈmægnɪtjuːd/
n. 重要性

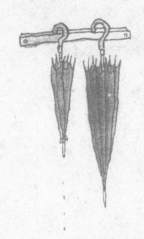

The lady and the lion

女士和狮子

A man whose stomach is filled can easily be won over.

吃饱了的男人很容易被征服。

A very talkative lady went to see the witch doctor[1] and told him her woes[1]. Once her husband was a loving man but now he does not care for her nor help in the house and all day long he goes out enjoying himself with friends. She went on and on repeating her problems. This was what the witch doctor advised her: "Go to the jungle and try and feed the lion. Don't come back until you've fed the lion, pet its head or pull its tail at the same time."

The lady went out searching for a lion. At last she saw a ferocious[3] lion roaming around looking for food but before she could throw the meat at the lion, it gave chase. The lady quickly climbed up the tree and trembled with fear. It was not until dark that the lion who was waiting at the foot of the tree went away. The same procedure[4] happened for many days. Strangely, after a week, the lion was appeared to wait for both the lady and her meat. It only gave out a slight growl[5] at the sight of her.

"How can I feed the lion, pet its head or pull its tail at the same time?" the lady moaned. As she sat at the treetop, she devised[6] many plans and at last came to a solution as to how to trap the lion without being hurt. The next day, the lady brought a huge trap-basket and before she approached the lion, she had roasted[7] the meat to add flavor[8] to the meat, as the smell would tickle the lion's appetite. She placed the meat right at the end corner of the trap. As soon as the lion saw the juicy meat, it hurriedly crawled[9] and put its head into the trap. The lady pulled the cord and closed up the trap. While the lion was enjoying the meat in the trap, the lady could not only pet its head but also tag its tail gently. She went

一个特爱唠叨的女士去拜访巫医，向他诉苦说她的丈夫曾经很爱她，但现在他不再爱她，也不帮她做家务，整天只是和朋友一块出去玩。她不停地在那儿说，巫医建议她："你到丛林中试着去喂一喂狮子，一定要等到喂完狮子再拍拍它的脑袋或拉拉它的尾巴之后才能回来。"

女士出去寻找狮子，最后她看到一头凶猛的狮子正在到处寻找食物。她还没有把肉扔给它，狮子就开始追她。女士迅速爬上了树，害怕得直打颤。直到天黑，在树底下等候的狮子才走开。同样的事情重演了好几天。奇怪的是，一星期后，狮子出现了，等着女士带肉来，而且看到她时也只是发出低沉的声音。

"我怎么去喂狮子呢，还要拍拍它的脑袋或拉拉它的尾巴？"女士埋怨说。当她坐在树顶时，她想了很多计划，最终想出了一个办法既能套住狮子又不受伤害。第二天，女士带了一个很大的篮子作为陷阱。她将肉烤得很香，这样会刺激狮子的食欲。她把肉放在陷阱的最里边。狮子一看到香喷喷的肉就马上爬过来，把头伸了进去。女士拉起绳子，将陷阱关好。当狮子在篮子里享受它的美味时，女士不仅可以拍它的脑袋，还可以轻轻地拉它的尾巴。她高兴地去找巫医，给他讲

❶ witch doctor
巫医
❷ woe /wəʊ/
n. 苦恼
❸ ferocious
/fəˈrəʊʃəs/
adj. 凶猛的
❹ procedure
/prəˈsiːdʒə(r)/
n. 程序
❺ growl /graʊl/
n. 低沉的吼声
❻ devise
/dɪˈvaɪz/
v. 想出，设计
❼ roast /rəʊst/
v. 烤
❽ flavor
/ˈfleɪvə(r)/
n. 香味
❾ crawl /krɔːl/
v. 爬

happily to the witch doctor and told him her success story.

"Lady, you've schemed and spent money and time to chop up the meat and roasted it each day. You've done so much for the lion! If only you can apply the same care for your husband and talk less, I am sure, he will be the same loving husband as before."

Chinese saying: A man whose stomach is filled can easily be won over[10].

她成功的经历。

　　"夫人，你制定了计划，每天花钱和时间来切肉、烤肉，你为狮子竟然做了那么多事！如果你也这样地关心你丈夫，少说话，我敢保证，他还会像以前一样爱你。"

　　中国俗语：吃饱了的男人很容易被征服。

⑩ win over
把…争取过来

The cat and the dog
who conquered the snake
战胜了蛇的猫和狗

A friend in need is a friend indeed and a cat and a dog could also be friends.

患难见真情，猫和狗也能成为好朋友。

There was an old lady who loved sitting by the fireside holding a book in her hand. She acquired the love of reading when she was young and this habit had stayed with her even at her old age. Her only married daughter who married a doctor lived with the old lady for a year or so. Later the doctor was posted to another country's hospital. "We both would love to have you stay with us, mother," her daughter said. "No, I will be an interfering mother-in-law and then your husband would hate me. You both come and visit me whenever you can. But when you are pregnant[1] with child I will, of course, go and stay with you as I look forward to seeing my grandchild."

There was logic in the old lady's thinking and she was happy to have her daughter and son-in-law visit her from time to time. As promised she would go to assist[2] her daughter during her confinement.[3] Time passed by and her daughter's family increased. "I now have four grandchildren," she would proudly tell her neighbor. They were childhood friends when young but over some silly misunderstanding both ladies hardly spoke to each other. During the school holidays, when the old lady's daughter and doctor husband were not traveling with their children to foreign lands, they would all visit her.

The old lady did not want any animals in the house. She once thought she would get a cat as a pet but no sooner had she heard the barking of the neighbor's dog, she would change her mind. "If I keep a cat and should the dog bark at her I would surely get annoyed[4]. I don't want any more trouble with my

老妇人喜欢坐在火边，手里拿一本书。她年轻时就喜欢读书，这个习惯一直保持到老。她惟一的女儿和一个医生结婚了，他们和她一起生活了一年左右，后来医生被派往另一个国家的医院工作。"我们两个都想和你生活在一起，妈妈。"她女儿说。"不，我不想做第三者，你的丈夫会恨我的。你们有时间就来看我吧，但是当你怀孕时，我当然会去和你们住在一起，盼着我的孙子出生。"

老妇人的想法很有道理，她很高兴女儿和女婿时时来看她，她也按许诺的那样在女儿分娩的时候去照顾她。时光飞逝，她女儿的孩子越来越多。"现在我有4个孙子了。"她很自豪地告诉她的邻居。她和邻居是儿时的朋友，但是因为一些小误会两个人几乎不怎么说话。学校放假期间，老人的女儿和当医生的丈夫不带孩子们去国外旅游时，他们就都来看她。

老人不喜欢屋子里有动物。她曾经想过养一只宠物猫，但她一听到邻居的狗叫就改变了想法。"如果我养一只猫，狗朝它叫时我肯定会很烦，我可不想和邻居再有任何摩擦。"

老妇人的房子周围有很多树，这房子是

① pregnant
/'pregnənt/
adj. 怀孕的

② assist /ə'sɪst/
v. 帮助

③ confinement
/kən'faɪnmənt/
n. 分娩

④ annoyed
/ə'nɔɪd/
adj. 烦人的

neighbor."

The old lady's house was surrounded with many trees. It was an old house she had inherited[5] from her parents. She was proud of her garden and had hired a gardener who kept the trees in shape[6] and the place clean. But the gardener was also getting aged as the old lady. Often he would fall sick and then the garden would be neglected[7]. The branches of the trees would crack[8] and overlap[9] each other, weeds sprung up[10] and the grass grew and gave out a dirty brownish color.

As the old lady's eyesight was getting dimmer, she could not see what was happening to the garden. She had a cozy[11] favorite spot in the garden. She would often sit under its shady tree for long hours, with a book in hand. Every now and then she would turn over the pages as if she was reading and let time pass her by.

This was how she spent her days.

One day as the old lady was sitting under the shadow of her favorite tree, she fell sound asleep. Her spectacles fell of her nose and the book rested on her lap[12]. As she slept, a rattlesnake[13] spied the old lady, and crawled out of the bushes quietly towards her. Its head held high and was prepared to dart forward and bite her.

But just at that moment, a cat that was resting on the bough of the tree saw what was happening. She waited till the snake was on the point of darting forward to bite, and then, jumping from

她的父母留给她的。她很为她的花园感到自豪，雇了一个园丁修剪树枝、打扫花园。但园丁也和老妇人一样上了年纪，经常会生病，花园便无人照看了。树枝会折断，或者互相交叉在一起，杂草疯长，弄得花园的颜色显得很脏。

老人视力越来越差，花园变成什么样她也看不到。在园子里，有一块非常舒服的地方，她经常在那儿的树阴下坐几个小时，手里拿着书。她不时地翻几页，好像在读书，以此消磨时间。这就是她打发时光的方式。

一天，老妇人坐在她最喜欢的树阴底下睡着了。眼镜从鼻梁上滑了下来，书摊在腿上。就在这个时候，一条暗中窥探的响尾蛇穿出灌木丛，并一声不响地向她爬去。它把头抬得很高，准备猛地窜向前咬她一口。

但是正在那时，一只在树干上休息的猫看到了发生的一切。它等到毒蛇猛地扑上去咬她的时候，突然从树干上飞快地跳下来，用爪子按住了蛇的头，但是狡猾的蛇不会轻易屈服。在一旁注视的邻居家的狗不停地叫，它冲过去迅速地咬住蛇的尾巴。

狗的叫喊声吵醒了老妇人，她很惊异地看到猫和狗正在和蛇做斗争。猫的爪子抓住蛇的头，狗的牙齿紧紧咬住蛇的尾巴。过了

❺ inherit
/ɪnˈherɪt/
v. 继承
❻ in shape
成型
❼ neglect
/nɪˈglekt/
v. 忽视
❽ crack /kræk/
v. 破裂
❾ overlap
/ˈəʊvəˈlæp/
v. 重叠
❿ spring up
疯长
⓫ cozy /ˈkəʊzɪ/
adj. 舒服的
⓬ lap /læp/
n. 大腿
⓭ rattlesnake
/ˈrætlsneɪk/
n. 响尾蛇

the bough, came swiftly and had her claws on the snake's head. But the wily snake would not give in so easily. The neighbor's dog that was watching kept on barking. It dashed out[14] and quickly bit the snake's tail.

The dog's barking awoke the old lady who was shocked to see the cat and dog struggling with the snake. The cat's claws was on the snake's head and the dog's teeth held tightly on to the snake's tail. It took a long while before the snake stopped wriggling[15] and laid dead.

The dog's master also rushed out to see what was happening. "Are you alright, Li Li," cried the neighbor, whose name was Lu Ping. It was a long time since the old lady heard her name being called. "Yes, thank you, Lu Ping. I am okay, your dog is very brave."

As Lu Ping took hold of her dog and it gave out a loud "woh, woh" bark. "This is the sweetest barking I've heard," said Li Li, the old lady. She then carried the cat and said, "You will be my pet from onwards." The cat cried out "meow, meow" and slept happily in the old lady's arms.

"Your dog and this cat saved my life," Li Li told her neighbor Lu Ping.

Li Li and Lu Ping became the best neighbors and renewed their friendship.

很长时间，蛇才停止挣扎，最后死了。

　　狗的主人也冲出来看发生了什么事。"你还好吧？丽丽。"邻居卢萍问道。老妇人好长时间没听到邻居这样叫她了。"是的，谢谢，卢萍，我很好，你的狗真勇敢。"

　　卢萍抱起狗时，狗发出"汪汪"的声音。"这是我听到的最好听的声音。"老妇人丽丽说。她抱起猫说，"从现在起我要你做我的宠物。"猫"喵喵"地叫着，躺在老妇人的胳膊里高兴地睡着了。

　　"你的狗和这只猫救了我的命。"丽丽告诉她的邻居卢萍。

　　丽丽和卢萍成了最好的邻居，又重新开始了她们的友谊。

⑭ **dash out**
冲出去
⑮ **wriggling**
/ˈrɪglɪŋ/
v. 蠕动

Gifts of love

爱的礼物

I left crying; I felt as if my life had been changed forever.

我哭着离开了，感觉我的生命也从此被改变了。

On the last day before Christmas, I hurried to the supermarket to buy the remaining gifts I hadn't managed to get earlier. When I saw all the people there, I started to mutter[1] to myself:

"It's going to take forever here and I still have so many other places to go ... Christmas really is getting more and more annoying every year. How I wish I could just lie down, go to sleep and only wake up after it's over ..."

Nonetheless, I made my way to the toy section[2], and there, I started to curse[3] the prices as I wondered if kids really played with such expensive toys. While looking around the shelves, I noticed a boy of about five, pressing a doll against his chest.

He kept touching the hair of the doll and looked quite sad. I wondered who the doll was for. Then the boy turned to an old woman beside him:

"Granny, are you sure I don't have enough money?" She replied, "You know that you don't have enough to buy this doll, my dear."

Then she asked him to stay there for five minutes while she looked around. She left quickly and the boy continued to hold the doll in his hand. I walked towards him and asked who he wished to give the doll to.

"It is the doll my sister loved most and wanted so much for

圣诞节前一天，我匆匆到超市去买早些时候还没买上的礼物。当我看见很多人在那时，我咕哝着对自己说："在这还要呆很长时间，而我还有很多地方要去……每年的圣诞节真是越来越烦人，我多么希望我能躺下来，睡觉，等到它结束了我再醒来……"

尽管如此，我还是挤着走到玩具部，在那儿，我又开始抱怨价格，我怀疑小孩根本就不会真的玩这些昂贵的玩具。我顺着货架到处看的时候，发现一个 5 岁的小男孩把洋娃娃紧紧抱在胸前。

他不停地摸洋娃娃的头发，看起来很伤心。我很好奇他会把洋娃娃送给谁。男孩转过身对旁边的老妇人说：

"奶奶，你确信我没有足够的钱吗？"奶奶说："亲爱的，你知道你没有足够的钱买这个洋娃娃的。"

于是她叫他在这呆 5 分钟，她四处再去看看。她很快离开了，男孩还是把那个洋娃娃握在手中。我向他走过去，问他想把洋娃娃送给谁。

"这是我妹妹最喜欢的洋娃娃，圣诞节她想要。她相信圣诞老人会给她的。"

我告诉他说圣诞老人最终会给她的，不用担心，但是他伤心地说："不，圣诞老人

① mutter
/ˈmʌtə(r)/
v. 咕哝
② section
/ˈsekʃən/
n. 部分
③ curse /kɜːs/
v. 诅咒，抱怨

Christmas. She was so sure that <u>Santa Claus</u>⁴ would bring it to her. "

I told him that maybe Santa Claus would bring it after all, and not to worry. But he said sadly, "No, Santa Claus cannot take it where she is now. My sister has gone to be with God. Daddy says mummy will also go to see God very soon, so I thought that she could take the doll with her to give my sister. "

My heart nearly stopped. The boy looked up at me and added, "I told daddy to tell mummy not to go yet. I asked him to wait until I'm back from the supermarket." Then he showed me a nice photo in which he was laughing.

"I also want mummy to take this photo with her so that she will not forget me. I love my mummy and I wish she didn't have to leave me. But daddy says she has to go to be with my little sister."

Then he looked again at the doll, silently. I quickly reached for my wallet, took out a few notes and said to him, "what if we checked again just in case you have enough money ? "

"Okay," he replied. I added some of my money to his without his noticing, and we started counting. There was enough for the doll, and some change.

The boy looked at me and said, "Last night, before going to bed, I asked God to make sure I have enough money to buy this

不能送到她现在所在的地方。我妹妹随着上帝走了。爸爸说妈妈也将很快去见上帝，我想妈妈可以把这个洋娃娃带给我妹妹。"

我的心几乎停止跳动了。小男孩看着我接着说："我叫爸爸告诉妈妈先不要去，等我从超市回来。"接着他给我看了一张漂亮的照片，照片上他笑得很灿烂。

"我还想让妈妈把照片带着，不要忘记我。我爱妈妈，不希望她离开我，但是爸爸说她要去陪我妹妹。"

他又看了一眼洋娃娃，没做声。我马上伸手去拿我的钱包，拿出几张钱后对他说："我们再来数数，看你的钱够不够？"

"好的，"他说。我趁他不注意把几张钱塞进他的钱里面，然后我们开始数，这下买洋娃娃的钱够了，还有一些剩余。

男孩看着我说："昨晚睡觉前我祈求上帝让我有足够的钱买这个洋娃娃，然后妈妈可以带给我妹妹。上帝听到了。"

"我还想有一些钱给我妈妈买一枝白玫瑰，但是我没有向上帝要得更多。你知道，我妈妈喜欢白玫瑰。"

过了几分钟，老奶奶回来了。我推着购物车走了，我带着和刚开始完全不同的心情买完了东西。那个小男孩的影子始终在我

doll so mummy can give it to my sister. He heard me.

"I also wanted some money to buy a white rose for my mummy, but I didn't dare ask God for too much. You know, my mummy loves white roses. "

A few minutes later, the old lady came again and I left with my trolley[5]. I finished my shopping in a totally different state from when I started. I couldn't get the boy out of my mind.

Then I remembered a newspaper report from two days back, about a drunk man in a truck who had hit a car driven by a young woman, who was with her little girl. The girl died instantly and the mother is now in a coma. Is this the family of the little boy?

Two days after our encounter in the supermarket, I read that the young mother had died.

I couldn't stop myself; I bought a bunch of white roses and went to the mortuary[6], where her body lay for visitors to pay their last respects. She was in her coffin, with a beautiful white rose in her hand and the photo of the boy and the doll over her chest. I left crying; I felt as if my life had been changed forever.

To this day, I find it hard to imagine the love the boy had for his mother and sister. But in a split second[7], a drunken driver took them away from him.

脑海里，挥之不去。

　　然后我记起了前两天在报纸上看过的一则报道，说是一个卡车司机酒后驾车，撞到了一辆小汽车，车上是一位年轻的妈妈和她的小女儿。小女孩当场就死了，妈妈现在处于昏迷状态。她们会不会就是这个小男孩的家人呢？

　　在超市遇到小男孩两天后，我在报纸上看到年轻妈妈去世了。

　　我不能自己，买了一束白玫瑰来到她的灵堂，在那里来访者向死者做最后的道别。她躺在棺材里，手上拿着漂亮的白色玫瑰花，胸脯上放着小男孩的照片和那个洋娃娃。我哭着离开了，感觉我的生命也从此被改变了。

　　直到今天，我还是难以想像小男孩对他妈妈和妹妹的爱，但始料不及的是，一个酒后驾车的司机把他们从他身边夺走了。

❺ trolley /'trɒlɪ/
n. 购物车
❻ mortuary
/'mɔːtjʊərɪ/
n. 太平间
❼ in a split second
瞬间，一刹那

Teddy

特　迪

Please remember that wherever you go, and whatever you do, you will have the opportunity to touch and/ or change a person's outlook. Please try to do it in a positive way.

请记住，不管你到哪儿，不管你做什么，你都有可能影响或改变一个人的前途。请以一种积极的态度去做。

Her name was Mrs. Thompson. As she stood in front of her 5th grade class on the very first day of school, she told the children a lie. Like most teachers, she looked at her students and said that she loved them all the same.

But that was impossible, because there in the front row, slumped[1] in his seat, was a little boy named Teddy Stoddard.

Mrs. Thompson had watched Teddy the year before and noticed that he didn't play well with the other children, that his clothes were messy and that he constantly needed a bath. And Teddy could be unpleasant. It got to the point[2] where Mrs. Thompson would actually take delight in marking his papers with a broad red pen, making bold X's and then putting a big "F" at the top of his papers.

At the school where Mrs. Thompson taught, she was required to review each child's past records and she put Teddy's off until last. However, when she reviewed his file, she was in for a surprise.

Teddy's first grade teacher wrote, "Teddy is a bright child with a ready laugh. He does his work neatly and has good manners ... he is a joy to be around."

His second grade teacher wrote, "Teddy is an excellent student, well liked by his classmates, but he is troubled because his mother has a terminal[3] illness and life at home must be a struggle."

她是汤普森夫人，第一天上课站在五年级学生面前时，她向孩子们撒了一个谎。像大多数老师一样，她看着学生说，她爱他们每一个人。

但是那是不可能的，因为在前排的一个名叫特迪的小男孩，老是趴在桌子上。

汤普森夫人前一年就注意到特迪和其他小孩相处不好，衣服很乱，经常不洗澡。可以说他很不讨人喜欢。这样说正好讲到正题了。汤普森夫人实际上很高兴用粗红笔改他的试卷，只需打上粗粗的红叉，然后在试卷上方大大地写上"F"。

汤普森夫人所在的学校要求老师查看每个小孩过去的记录。她最后才看特迪的，然而当她看他的档案时，大吃了一惊。

特迪一年级的老师写道："特迪很聪明，喜欢笑，作业很工整，很有教养……经常给周围的人带来欢乐。"

二年级的老师写道："特迪很优秀，同学们很喜欢他，但是他遇到了不幸，因为他妈妈的病到了晚期，他家的生活一定很艰辛。"

三年级的老师写道："妈妈的去世给他带来很大的打击。他尽最大努力从痛苦中走出来，但他的爸爸从不关心他，如果不采取

❶ slump /slʌmp/
v. 沉重地落下或倒下

❷ get to the point
谈到正题

❸ terminal
/'tɜːmɪnl/
adj. 晚期

His third grade teacher wrote, "His mother's death had been hard on him. He tries to do his best, but his father doesn't show much interest and his home life will soon affect him if some steps aren't taken."

Teddy's fourth grade teacher wrote, "Teddy is withdrawn[4] and doesn't show much interest in school. He doesn't have many friends and he sometimes sleeps in class".

By now, Mrs. Thompson realized the problem and she was ashamed of herself. She felt even worse when her students brought her Christmas presents, wrapped in beautiful ribbons and bright paper, except for Teddy's.

His present was clumsily[5] wrapped in the heavy, brown paper that he got from a grocery bag. Mrs. Thompson took pains to open it in the middle of the other presents. Some of the children started to laugh when she found a rhinestone[6] bracelet[7] with some of the stones missing, and a bottle that was one quarter full of perfume. But she stifled[8] the children's laughter when she exclaimed[9] how pretty the bracelet was, putting it on, and dabbing[10] some of the perfume[11] on her wrist. Teddy Stoddard stayed after school that day just long enough to say, "Mrs. Thompson, today you smelled just like my Mom used to."

After the children left she cried for at least an hour. On that very day, she quit teaching reading, and writing, and arithmetic[12]. Instead, she began to teach children. Mrs. Thompson paid particular

措施的话，不久他的家庭生活将会给他带来不利影响。"

特迪四年级的老师写道："特迪很孤僻，对学校不太感兴趣。他朋友不多，有时还在课堂上睡觉。"

现在，汤普森夫人现在意识到了问题之所在，为自己感到羞耻。当她的学生给她送来的圣诞礼物都包在亮丽的彩纸里，系着漂亮的彩带，而惟独特迪的不是时，她更感到不舒服了。

他的礼物是用从杂货袋上剪下来的厚厚的牛皮纸笨拙地包起来的。和其他礼物相比，汤普森夫人费了很大的劲才打开它。里面有一串掉了几粒石头的莱茵石手镯，还有一瓶只剩下四分之一的香水。一些小孩看到这些都笑了。她制止了孩子们的嘲笑，称赞说这个手镯是多么的漂亮，并把它戴上，而且还在手腕上擦了一点香水。那天特迪放学后等了好长时间，终于鼓起勇气对老师说："汤普森夫人，今天你身上的香味和我妈妈以前的一样。"

孩子们离开后她哭了一个多小时。那天，她没有教阅读、写作、算术，而是开始教育孩子们。汤普森夫人尤其注意特迪，当她教他的时候，他的大脑似乎活跃起来，她

④ **withdrawn**
/wɪðˈdrɔːn/
adj. 孤僻的

⑤ **clumsily**
/ˈklʌmzɪlɪ/
adv. 笨拙地

⑥ **rhinestone**
/ˈraɪnstəʊn/
n. 莱茵石

⑦ **bracelet**
/ˈbreɪslɪt/
n. 手镯

⑧ **stifle** /ˈstaɪfl/
v. 感到窒息

⑨ **exclaim**
/ɪksˈkleɪm/
v. 惊叫

⑩ **dab** /dæb/
v. 擦

⑪ **perfume**
/ˈpɜːfjuːm/
n. 香水

⑫ **arithmetic**
/əˈrɪθmətɪk/
n. 算术

attention to Teddy. As she worked with him, his mind seemed to come alive. The more she encouraged him, the faster he responded.

By the end of the year, Teddy had become one of the smartest children in the class and, despite her lie that she would love all the children the same, Teddy became one of her "teacher's pets."

A year later, she found a note under her door, from Teddy, telling her that she was still the best teacher he ever had in his whole life. Six years went by before she got another note from Teddy. He then wrote that he had finished high school, third in his class, and she was still the best teacher he ever had in his whole life.

Four years after that, she got another letter, saying that while things had been tough at times, he'd stayed in school, had stuck with it, and would soon graduate from college with the highest of honors.

He assured Mrs. Thompson that she was still the best and favorite teacher he ever had in his whole life. Then four more years passed and yet another letter came. This time he explained that after he got his bachelor's[13] degree, he decided to go a little further.

The letter explained that she was still the best and favorite teacher he ever had. But now his name was a little longer—the letter was signed, Theodore F. Stoddard, MD.

越鼓励他，他反应得越快。

　　到年末时，特迪成了全班最聪明的小孩之一。尽管她曾撒谎说她爱每一个学生，但是特迪最终成了她的一颗"掌上明珠"。

　　一年以后，她发现她门下有一张纸条，是特迪写的，他说，她是他一生中遇到的最好的老师。6年后，她又收到特迪的一张纸条，告诉她说他完成了高中学业，得了第三名，她依然是他一生中遇到的最好的老师。

　　4年后，她又收到一封信，说尽管过得很艰难，他还是坚持在学校学习，他马上就要以优异的成绩大学毕业了。

　　他向汤普森夫人坚定地说，她依然是他一生中遇到的最好的老师。4年多后特迪又寄来一封信，这次他说在拿到学士学位后又决定继续深造了。

　　这封信还说她依然是他一生中遇到的最好的老师。但是现在他的名字变得长了一些——西奥多·斯托达德，医学博士。

　　故事还没有结束。那年春天又寄来一封信，特迪说他遇到一个女孩，准备结婚了。他解释说他爸爸前年去世了，他问汤普森夫人是否同意在婚礼上坐在本应属于新郎母亲的座位上。当然，汤普森夫人同意了。

　　猜猜发生了什么？她戴上掉了几粒莱茵

⑲ bachelor
/ˈbætʃələ(r)/
n. 文理学士

The story doesn't end there. You see, there was yet another letter that spring. Teddy said he'd met this girl and was going to be married. He explained that his father had died a couple of years ago and he was wondering if Mrs. Thompson might agree to sit in the place at the wedding that was usually reserved for the mother of the groom. Of course, Mrs. Thompson did.

And guess what? She wore that bracelet, the one with several rhinestones missing. And she made sure she was wearing the perfume that Teddy remembered his mother wearing on their last Christmas together.

They hugged each other, and Dr. Stoddard whispered[14] in Mrs. Thompson's ear, "Thank you Mrs. Thompson for believing in me. Thank you so much for making me feel important and showing me that I could make a difference." Mrs. Thompson, with tears in her eyes, whispered back. She said, "Teddy, you have it all wrong. You were the one who taught me that I could make a difference. I didn't know how to teach until I met you."

Please remember that wherever you go, and whatever you do, you will have the opportunity to touch and/or change a person's outlook[15]. Please try to do it in a positive way.

"Friends are angels who lift us to our feet when our wings have trouble remembering how to fly."

It makes you wonder how many "Teddy's" out there might have been missed.

石的手镯，还抹了香水，就是特迪记得的最后一次和妈妈圣诞聚会时妈妈抹的香水的味道。

　　他们拥抱在一起，斯托达德博士在汤普森夫人耳边低声说："汤普森夫人，谢谢你相信我。非常感谢你使我有了自信，告诉我能改变自己的生活。"汤普森夫人眼里噙着眼泪说："特迪，你弄错了，是你教给我重要的启示。直到遇到你我才知道怎么教学。"

　　请记住，不管你到哪儿，不管你做什么，你都有可能影响或改变一个人的前途。请以一种积极的态度去做。

　　"朋友是天使，当我们的翅膀不能飞时，是朋友帮助我们站立起来。"

　　你可能会问：有多少个特迪被忽视了呢？

⓮ whisper
/ˈhwɪspə(r)/
v. 低声说
⓯ outlook
/ˈaʊtlʊk/
n. 前途

In life, we are happiest when ...

生活中当我们最幸福时…

In life, there are enough times when we are disappointed, depressed and annoyed. We don't really have to go looking for them. We have a wonderful world that is full of beauty, light and promise.

生命中我们有很多的失望、沮丧和烦恼，我们根本不需要寻找。我们美妙的世界充满了美丽、光明、希望。

A man and his girlfriend were married. It was a large celebration[1].

All of their friends and family came to see the lovely ceremony[2] and to partake of the festivities[3] and celebrations. All had a wonderful time.

The bride was gorgeous[4] in her white wedding gown[5] and the groom was very dashing[6] in his black tuxedo[7]. Everyone could tell that the love they had for each other was true.

A few months later, the wife came to the husband with a proposal[8], "I read in a magazine, a while ago, about how we can strengthen our marriage," she offered.

"Each of us will write a list of the things that we find a bit annoying with the other person. Then, we can talk about how we can fix them together and make our lives happier together."

The husband agreed. So each of them went to a separate room in the house and thought of the things that annoyed them about the other. They thought about this question for the rest of the day and wrote down what they came up with[9].

The next morning, at the breakfast table, they decided that they would go over their lists.

"I'll start," offered the wife. She took out her list. It had many

一个男人和他的女朋友结婚，举行了一场盛大的结婚庆典。

所有的朋友和家人都来到结婚典礼上参加欢宴和庆祝活动。大家都过得很开心。

穿着白色婚纱的新娘漂亮迷人，穿着黑色礼服的新郎英俊潇洒。每个人都能看出他们彼此的爱是真诚的。

几个月后，妻子走近丈夫提议说："我刚才在杂志上看到一篇文章，说的是怎样巩固婚姻。"她说，"我们两个人都各自把对方的小毛病列在一张纸上，然后我们商量一下怎样解决，以便使我们的生活更幸福。"

丈夫同意了。于是他们各自走向不同的房间去想对方的缺点。那一天余下的时间里，他们都在思考这个问题，并且把他们想到的都写下来。

第二天早上，吃早饭的时候，他们决定谈谈彼此的缺点。"我先开始吧。"妻子说。她拿出她的单子，上面列举了很多条，事实上，足足写满了3页。当她开始念的时候，她注意到丈夫眼里含着泪花。

"怎么啦?"她问。"没什么。"丈夫答道，"继续念吧。"

妻子又接着念。整整三满页都念完之后她把单子整齐地放在桌上，两手交叉放在上

---

❶ celebration
/ˌselɪˈbreɪʃən/
n. 庆祝

❷ ceremony
/ˈserɪmənɪ/
n. 典礼，仪式

❸ festivity
/fesˈtɪvətɪ/
n. 庆祝活动

❹ gorgeous
/ˈɡɔːdʒəs/
adj. 极好的

❺ gown /ɡaʊn/
n. 长袍

❻ dashing
/ˈdæʃɪŋ/
adj. 时髦的

❼ tuxedo
/tʌkˈsiːdəʊ/
n. 礼服

❽ proposal
/prəˈpəʊzəl/
n. 建议

❾ come up with
想出

items on it. Enough to fill 3 pages, in fact. As she started reading the list of the little annoyances, she noticed that tears were starting to appear in her husband's eyes.

"What's wrong?" she asked. "Nothing," the husband replied, "keep reading your list."

The wife continued to read until she had read all three pages to her husband. She neatly placed her list on the table and folded[10] her hands over the top of it.

"Now, you read your list and then we'll talk about the things on both of our lists," She said happily.

Quietly the husband stated, "I don't have anything on my list. I think that you are perfect the way that you are. I don't want you to change anything for me. You are lovely and wonderful and I wouldn't want to try and change anything about you."

The wife, touched by his honesty and the depth of his love for her and his acceptance of her, turned her head and wept.

In life, there are enough times when we are disappointed, depressed and annoyed. We don't really have to go looking for them. We have a wonderful world that is full of beauty, light and promise. Why waste time in this world looking for the bad, disappointing or annoying when we can look around us, and see the wondrous[11] things before us?

面。

　　"现在该你念了，然后我们谈谈所列举的缺点。"她高兴地说。

　　丈夫平静地说："我什么也没写，我觉得像你这样就很完美了，我不想让你为我改变什么。你很可爱迷人，我不想让你改变。"

　　妻子被丈夫的诚实和对她深深的爱和接纳感动了，她转过头去哭起来。

　　生命中我们有很多的失望、沮丧和烦恼，我们根本不需要寻找。我们美妙的世界充满了美丽、光明、希望。但是，当我们放眼四周时，为什么浪费时间寻找不快、失望和烦恼，而看不到我们面前的美好事物呢？

⑩ **fold** /fəʊld/
v. 合拢
⑪ **wondrous**
/ˈwʌndrəs/
adj. 极好的

Life

生 活

A bumblebee, if drops into an open tumbler, will be there until it dies, unless it is taken out.

一只大黄蜂如果掉进一个敞口的平底大玻璃杯里，除非它被救出来，否则只能等死。

If you put a buzzard[1] in a pen that is 6 feet by 8 feet and is entirely open at the top, the bird, in spite of its ability to fly, will be an absolute prisoner. The reason is that a buzzard always begins a flight from the ground with a run of 10 to 12 feet. Without space to run, as is its habit[2], it will not even attempt to fly, but will remain a prisoner for life in a small jail with no top.

The ordinary bat that flies around at night, a remarkably nimble[3] creature in the air, cannot take off from a level place. If it is placed on the floor or flat ground, all it can do is shuffle[4] about helplessly and, no doubt, painfully, until it reaches some slight elevation from which it can throw itself into the air. Then, at once, it takes off like a flash[5].

A bumblebee[6], if drops into an open tumbler[7], will be there until it dies, unless it is taken out. It never sees the means of escape at the top, but persists in trying to find some way out through the sides near the bottom. It will seek a way where none exists, until it completely destroys itself.

In many ways, there are lots of people like the buzzard, the bat and the bumblebee. They are struggling about with all their problems and frustrations, not ever realizing that the answer is always ABOVE.

Look up, say a little prayer[8] and take off.

如果把一只蜂鹰放在一个长 8 英尺、宽 6 英尺，顶完全敞开的围栏里，尽管它能飞，但最终也会变成一个绝对的囚禁者。原因是蜂鹰经常跑 10 到 12 英尺后开始从地面起飞，跑是它的习惯。没有空间跑，它甚至不会试着去飞，而是留在没有顶的小监狱里，终生为囚徒。

晚上到处飞，而且在空中特别机敏的动物——蝙蝠，不能从平地上起飞。如果把它放在地板上或平地上，它只能无助地拖着步子，无疑很痛苦，直到把它放到稍微高一点的地方才能飞向天空。那时，它立即像闪电一般起飞。

一只大黄蜂如果掉进一个敞口的平底大玻璃杯里，除非它被救出来，否则只能等死。它从来看不到上面的出路，只是坚持在瓶底周围的边上寻找出路。实际上那里根本没有出路，所以，它最终毁灭了自己。

在很多方面，很多人都像蜂鹰、蝙蝠和大黄蜂一样。他们在烦恼、沮丧中挣扎，却从来没有意识到答案总是"向上"。

向上看，为自己祈祷，然后起飞。

❶ **buzzard**
/ˈbʌzəd/
n. 蜂鹰

❷ **habit**
/ˈhæbɪt/
n. 习惯

❸ **nimble**
/ˈnɪmbl/
adj. 敏捷的

❹ **shuffle**
/ˈʃʌfl/
v. 拖着步子走

❺ **flash** /flæʃ/
n. 闪电

❻ **bumblebee**
/ˈbʌmblbiː/
n. 大黄蜂

❼ **tumbler**
/ˈtʌmblə(r)/
n. 平底玻璃杯

❽ **prayer**
/preə(r)/
n. 祈祷

Little boy and ice cream

小男孩和冰激凌

He couldn't have the sundae, because he had to have enough left to leave her a tip.

他不能吃圣代，因为他必须省下钱来给她小费。

In the days when an ice cream sundae[1] cost much less, a 10-year-old boy entered a hotel coffee shop and sat at a table. A waitress put a glass of water in front of him.

"How much is an ice cream sundae?" he asked. "Fifty cents," replied the waitress. The little boy pulled his hand out of his pocket and studied the coins in it. "Well, how much is a plain dish of ice cream?" he inquired.

By now more people were waiting for a table and the waitress was growing impatient. "Thirty-five cents," she brusquely[2] replied.

The little boy again counted his coins. "I'll have the plain ice cream," he said. The waitress brought the ice cream, put the bill on the table and walked away.

The boy finished the ice cream, paid the cashier and left. When the waitress came back, she began to cry as she wiped down the table.

There, placed beside the empty dish, were two nickels[3] and five pennies[4] —You see, he couldn't have the sundae, because he had to have enough left to leave her a tip[5].

The moral of the story: Don't underestimate any one even if he is a little child.

在冰激凌圣代还不贵的时候，有一个10岁的小男孩走进一家酒店咖啡馆，坐在桌子旁。一个服务小姐端了一杯水放在他面前。

"冰激淋圣代多少钱?"他问。"50美分。"服务小姐说。小男孩把手从口袋里拿出来，数了数手里的钱。"那么一个普通的冰激凌呢?"他问道。

这时候，等座位的人越来越多，服务小姐显得不耐烦了。"35美分。"她粗鲁地回答道。

小男孩又数了数他的硬币。"我要一个普通的冰激凌。"他说。服务小姐拿来冰激凌，把账单放在桌上，就离开了。

小孩吃完冰激凌，付了钱走了。当服务小姐回来擦桌子时，她哭了。

空盘子旁边放着2个5分的镍币和5便士。他不能吃圣代，因为他必须省下钱来给她小费。

这个故事的寓意是：不要小瞧任何人，即便他是个小孩。

❶ sundae
/ˈsʌndɪ/
n. 圣代(食品)

❷ brusquely
/brʊsklɪ/
adv. 粗暴地

❸ nickel /ˈnɪkl/
n. 镍币

❹ penny /ˈpenɪ/
n. 便士

❺ tip /tɪp/
n. 小费

May you

希望你……

These things I wish for you—tough times and disappointment, hard work and happiness. To me, it's the only way to appreciate life.

我希望你拥有这些东西———艰难时刻和失望，努力工作和幸福。对我来说，这是惟一享受生活的方式。

We tried so hard to make things better for our kids that we made them worse. For my grandchildren, I'd like better.

I'd really like for them to know about hand me down clothes and homemade ice cream and leftover[1] meat loaf[2] sandwiches. I really would.

I hope you learn humility[3] by being humiliated, and that you learn honesty by being cheated.

I hope you learn to make your own bed and mow the lawn and wash the car. And I really hope nobody gives you a brand new car when you are sixteen.

It will be good if at least one time you can see puppies born and your old dog put to sleep. I hope you get a black eye fighting for something you believe in. I hope you have to share a bedroom with your younger brother/sister. And it's all right if you have to draw a line down the middle of the room, but when he wants to crawl under the covers with you because he's scared[4], I hope you let him. When you want to see a movie and your little brother/sister wants to <u>tag along</u>[5], I hope you'll let him/her.

I hope you have to walk uphill to school with your friends and that you live in a town where you can do it safely. On rainy days when you have to catch a ride, I hope you don't ask your driver to drop you two blocks away so you won't be seen riding with someone as uncool as your Mom.

我们很努力地为孩子们创造更好的生活，结果却更加糟糕。我希望我的孙子会好一些。

我真的希望他们了解家人传给我的衣服、自制的冰激凌、吃剩的夹肉三明治面包。我真的希望。

我希望你能通过贬低自己学会谦逊，被骗之后学到诚实。我希望你能自己整理床铺、修剪草坪、洗车。我也真的希望在你16岁时没人给你买心爱的小汽车。

至少有一次你能看到小狗出生，大狗被安顿好睡觉就太好了。我希望你即使被别人打得鼻青脸肿也坚持捍卫自己的信仰。我希望你能和你的弟弟或妹妹同住一间卧室。你要在中间划一条线也可以，但当他很害怕，要爬进你的被窝时，我希望你能让他进来。当你想去看电影，你的弟弟妹妹也要去时，我希望你能带上他们。

我希望你能吃点苦，和你的朋友走着去学校。你住在城镇里，这样做很安全。在下雨天，你必须搭自行车时，我希望你不要因为你不想让人看到你和像你妈妈这样一点都不酷的人骑一辆车，而让骑车人在两个街区之外把你放下来。

如果你想要一个投石器，我希望你的爸

❶ **leftover**
/ˈleftˌəʊvə(r)/
n. 剩余物
❷ **loaf** /ləʊf/
n. 一条面包
❸ **humility**
/hjuːˈmɪlətɪ/
n. 谦逊
❹ **scared** /skeəd/
adj. 惊吓，恐慌
❺ **tag along**
紧紧跟随

If you want a slingshot[6], I hope your Dad teaches you how to make one, instead of buying one, I hope you learn to dig in the dirt and read books.

When you learn to use computers, I hope you also learn to add and subtract[7] in your head. I hope your friends tease[8] you when you have your first crush[9] on a boy/girl, and when you talk back to your mother that you learn what ivory soap tastes like. May you skin your knee climbing a mountain, burn your hand on a stove and stick your tongue on a frozen flagpole[10].

I don't care if you try a beer once, but I hope you don't like it. And if a friend offers you dope[11] or a joint[12], I hope you realize he is not your friend. I sure hope you make time to sit on a porch[13] with your Grandma/Grandpa and go fishing with your Uncle.

May you feel sorrow at a funeral and joy during the holidays. I hope your mother punishes you when you throw a baseball through your neighbor's window and that she hugs you and kisses you at Christmas time when you give her a plaster mold[14] of your hand.

These things I wish for you—tough times and disappointment, hard work and happiness. To me, it's the only way to appreciate life.

Written with a pen. Sealed with a kiss. I'm here for you. And if I die before you do, I'll go to heaven and wait for you.

We secure our friends, not by accepting favors, but by doing them.

爸教你怎么做，而不是买一个。我希望你学会挖泥土，学会读书。

当你学电脑时，我希望你也学会用大脑进行加减运算。我希望当你迷恋一个男孩或女孩时，当你告诉你妈妈你知道了象牙牌肥皂是什么味道时，被你的朋友取笑。希望你爬山时擦破膝盖上的皮，烤火时烫伤手，希望你的舌头粘在冰凉的旗杆上。

我不在意你偶尔喝杯啤酒，但是我希望你不要沉迷。当一个朋友给你毒品或大麻烟卷时，我希望你能意识到他不是你的朋友。我也希望你能找个时间和你爷爷奶奶在走廊上坐坐，和叔叔去钓钓鱼。

希望你在葬礼上感到悲伤，在假期感到快乐。我希望当你扔棒球砸碎了邻居的窗子时，你妈妈惩罚你，也希望当你在圣诞节把你的石膏模具手送给她时，她又是抱你又是吻你。

我希望你拥有这些东西——艰难时刻和失望，努力工作和幸福。对我来说，这是惟一享受生活的方式。

用笔写信，用吻封缄。我为你活着。如果我比你先离开这个世界，我会到天堂去等你。

我们结交朋友，不是通过接受帮助，而是给予帮助。

⑥ **slingshot**
/ˈslɪŋʃɒt/
n. 投石器

⑦ **subtract**
/səbˈtrækt/
v. 减去

⑧ **tease** /tiːz/
v. 取笑

⑨ **crush** /krʌʃ/
v. 迷恋

⑩ **flagpole**
/ˈflæɡpəʊl/
n. 旗杆

⑪ **dope** /dəʊp/
n. 毒品

⑫ **joint** /dʒɔɪnt/
n. 含大麻的香烟

⑬ **porch** /pɔːtʃ/
n. 走道，门廊

⑭ **plaster mold**
石膏模具

Puppy love

最爱小狗

"Don't you remember? When I asked you one day what love is, you told me love depends on the sighs of your heart. The more you love, the bigger the sigh is!"

"你还记得吧，有一天我问你爱是什么时，你告诉我爱取决于你内心的叹息。你爱得越深，叹息越长！"

"Danielle keeps repeating it over and over again. We've been back to this animal shelter[1] at least five times. It has been weeks now since we started all of this," the mother told the volunteer.

"What is it she keeps asking for?" the volunteer asked. "Puppy[2] size!" replied the mother. "Well, we have plenty of puppies, if that's what she's looking for." "I know ... we have seen most of them," the Mom said in frustration[3] ...

Just then Danielle came walking into the office. "Well, did you find one?" asked her mom. "No, not this time," Danielle said with sadness in her voice. "Can we come back on the weekend?" The two women looked at each other, shook their heads and laughed. "You never know when we will get more dogs. Unfortunately, there's always a supply," the volunteer said.

Danielle took her mother by the hand and headed to the door. "Don't worry, I'll find one this weekend," she said. Over the next few days both mom and dad had long conversations with her. They both felt she was being too particular. "It's this weekend or we're not looking any more," Dad finally said in frustration. "We don't want to hear anything more about puppy size either," Mom added.

Sure enough, they were the first ones in the shelter on Saturday morning.

"丹妮尔老是到这个动物收容所来，这至少是第5次了。从我们第一次来算起，已经几个星期了。"妈妈告诉志愿工作者。

"她一直想要什么？"志愿工作者问道。"小狗。"妈妈答道。"我们这有很多小狗，看有没有她想要的。""我知道……我们已经看了很多了。"妈妈沮丧地说。

正在那时，丹妮尔走进办公室。"找到了吗？"妈妈问。"没有。这次还是没找到。"丹妮尔伤心地说。"我们周末能再来吗？"两位女士互相看着对方，摇了摇头，笑了。"你们不知道我们什么时候来更多的狗。不幸的是，经常会有供货。"志愿工作者说。

丹妮尔拉着妈妈的手向门走去。"不用担心，这个周末我们会找到一只的。"她说。接下来的几天妈妈和爸爸都找她长谈，他们都觉得她太挑剔了。"就这个周末，我们以后再也不找了。"爸爸最后灰心地说。"我们再也不要听到任何关于小狗的事情了。"妈妈补充道。

周六早上，当然他们是最早来到收容所的。

现在丹妮尔已经很熟悉周围的路了。她直接跑到关小狗的地方。每次都这样，妈妈

① shelter
/ˈʃeltə(r)/
n. 收容所

② puppy /ˈpʌpɪ/
n. 幼犬

③ frustration
/frʌˈtreɪʃən/
n. 沮丧

By now Danielle knew her way around, so she ran right for the section that housed the smaller dogs. Tired of the routine, mom sat in the small waiting room at the end of the first row of cages. There was an observation window so you could see the animals during times when visitors weren't permitted.

Danielle walked slowly from cage to cage, kneeling[4] periodically[5] to take a closer look. One by one the dogs were brought out and she held each one.

One by one she said, "Sorry, you're not the one." It was the last cage on this last day in search of the perfect pup. The volunteer opened the cage door and the child carefully picked up the dog and held it closely.

This time she took a little longer. "Mom, that's it! I found the right puppy! "

"He's the one! I know it!" she screamed with joy. "It's the puppy sighs!"

"But it's the same size as all the other puppies you held over the last few weeks," Mom said. "No, not size—the sighs. When I held him in my arms, he sighed," she said.

"Don't you remember? When I asked you one day what love is, you told me love depends on the sighs of your heart. The more you love, the bigger the sigh is!" The two women looked at each

厌烦了,于是她坐在第一排笼子尽头的一间小休息室里。游客不允许进去的时候可以从那里的观看窗看那些动物。

丹妮尔慢慢地从一个笼子走向另一个笼子。为了看得更清楚,她不停地跪下来把每一只狗拿出来抱抱。

每次她都说:"对不起,不是你。"那天是寻找完美小狗的最后一天,当她走到最后一个笼子时,志愿工作者拉开门,这个孩子小心地抓住一只狗,紧紧地抱着。

这一次她抱的时间长些。"妈妈,找到了,我找到我要的小狗了!"

"就是它,我知道!"她欢快地尖叫着。"就是这样的叹息!"

"但是这和你上几周抱的那些狗一样大啊。"妈妈说。

"不是大小——是叹息声。我把它抱在怀里时,它会叹息的。"她说。

"你还记得吧,有一天我问你爱是什么时,你告诉我爱取决于你内心的叹息。你爱得越深,叹息越长!"两人对视了一会儿。妈妈不知道是该哭还是该笑。当她弯腰拥抱孩子时,她哭了,也笑了。

"妈妈,每一次你抱我的时候,我都会叹息,你和爸爸工作回来彼此拥抱时也会叹息。

❹ kneel /niːl/
v. 屈膝跪下
❺ periodically
/ˌpɪərɪˈɒdɪkəlɪ/
adv. 定期地

other for a moment. Mom didn't know whether to laugh or cry. As she stooped[6] down to hug the child, she did a little of both.

"Mom, every time you hold me, I sigh. When you and Daddy come home from work and hug each other, you both sigh. I knew I would find the right puppy if it sighed when I held it in my arms," she said. Then holding the puppy up close to her face, she said, "Mom, he loves me. I heard the sighs of his heart!"

Close your eyes for a moment and think about the love that makes you sigh. I not only find it in the arms of my loved ones, but in the caress[7] of a sunset, the kiss of the moonlight and the gentle brush of cool air on a hot day.

They are the sighs of God. Take the time to stop and listen; you will be surprised at what you hear. "Life is not measured by the breaths we take, but by the moments that take our breath away[8]."

Hugs and sighs.

我知道我要找的小狗是我抱它时，它也叹息。"她说。她把小狗紧紧贴在脸上说："妈妈，它爱我，我听见它内心的叹息声了！"

把眼睛闭上一会，想一想使你叹息的爱。我不仅能在爱人的怀抱里找到，而且也能在落日的爱抚中、月光的亲吻中、热天里凉风的微抚中找到。那是上帝的叹息。花点时间停下来听听，你会惊奇于你所听到的。"生命不是以我们的呼吸，而是通过情感来衡量的"。

拥抱，叹息！

❻ stoop /stu:p/

v. 弯腰

❼ caress /kə'res/

n. 抚摸

❽ take one's breath away

使某人激动得透不过气来

Rods

窗帘杆

When she had finished, she went into each room and deposited a few of the half-eaten shrimp shells into the hollow of the curtain rods. She then cleaned up the kitchen and left.

吃完之后，她走到每一个房间，把吃了一半的虾塞进窗帘杆里，然后收拾好厨房离开了。

A man dumped his wife for a younger woman.

He wanted to continue living in their downtown luxury apartment with his new lover, so he asked his wife to move out and get another place.

His wife agreed to this, provided that he would give her 3 days alone at the apartment to pack up her things. She spent the first day packing her belongings into boxes, crates[1] and suitcases. On the second day, she had the movers come and collect her things.

On the third day, she sat down for the last time at their beautiful dining table by candlelight, put on some soft background music, and feasted on a pound of shrimp and a bottle of Chardonnay[2]. When she had finished, she went into each room and deposited[3] a few of the half-eaten shrimp shells into the hollow of the curtain rods. She then cleaned up the kitchen and left.

When the husband returned with his new lover, all was bliss[4] for the first few days. Then slowly the apartment began to smell. They tried everything; cleaning and mopping[5] and airing the place out. Vents[6] were checked for dead rodents[7], carpets were steam cleaned. Air fresheners were hung everywhere.

Exterminators[8] were brought in to <u>set off</u>[9] gas canisters[10], during which they had to move out for a few days, and in the end they even paid to replace the expensive carpet.

一个男人抛弃妻子，投入另一个年轻女人的怀抱。

他想和情人继续住在市中心的豪华公寓里，于是，他叫妻子搬出去到另一个地方住。

妻子同意了，要求他只给她3天时间，让她一个人在公寓里收拾她的东西。第一天，她把她所有的东西装进盒子、大木箱、手提箱里。第二天，她叫搬运工人搬走了。

第三天，她最后一次坐在燃着烛光的精致饭桌旁，伴着柔美的音乐，吃了一磅虾，喝了一瓶夏敦埃酒。吃完之后，她走到每一个房间，把吃了一半的虾塞进窗帘杆里，然后收拾好厨房离开了。

回来后的最初几天，丈夫和情人过着神仙般的日子。慢慢地房子里开始散发出气味。他们想尽了一切办法，清扫、拖地、消除房间的异味。钻孔看是否有死老鼠，地毯用蒸汽清洗了，到处都挂着空气清新剂。

除味器也被搬进屋里消除气味，这段时间他们只有搬出去住几天，最后甚至花钱换掉了昂贵的地毯。

最后，他们再也不能忍受了，决定搬家。因为房子散发出难闻的气味没有一个人买，于是他们只得向银行贷一大笔钱买新家。

搬家公司来了，他们很专业地做了打包工

❶ crate /kreɪt/
n. 大木箱

❷ Chardonnay
/ˌʃɑːdənˈeɪ/
n. 夏敦埃酒

❸ deposit
/dɪˈpɒzɪt/
v. 存，放

❹ bliss /blɪs/
n. 极乐

❺ mop /mɒp/
v. 拖地

❻ vent /vent/
n. 孔，口

❼ rodent
/ˈrəʊdənt/
n. 啮齿动物

❽ exterminator
/ɪkˈstɜːmɪneɪtə(r)/
n. 毁灭，消除

❾ set off
抵消，消除

❿ canister
/ˈkænɪstə(r)/
n. 小罐

Finally, they could not take it any longer and decided to move. They could not find a buyer for their stinky[11] apartment, so they had to borrow a huge sum of money from the bank to purchase a new place.

The moving company arrived and did a very professional packing job, taking everything to their new home ... Including the curtain rods.

作，把所有的东西都搬到新家——包括那些窗帘杆。

⓫ **stinky** /ˈstɪŋkɪ/
adj. 发臭的，难闻的

Story of our life

生命的故事

God, being good-natured, agreed with a smile.

上帝好心，笑着同意了。

In the beginning, in China, God created[1] the cow. He said to the creature, "Ah Ngau (cow), your job is to go to the field with the farmer all day long. You will have the energy[2] to pull things. You will also provide milk for the people to drink. You are to work all day under the sun. In return[3], you will only eat grass. For that, you will have a lifespan of 50 years."

Ah Ngau objected[4]. "What? I have to work all day in the sun and only get to eat grass? On top of that, I have to give my milk away. This is tough and you want me to live 50 years. I'll take 20 and you can have the remaining 30 years back!"

God agreed.

On the second day, God created the dog. He said, "Ah Kow (dog), I created you for a purpose. You are to sit all day by the door of your master's house. Should anyone come near, you are to bark at him. In return, you will eat your master's leftovers. I'll give you a lifespan of 20 years."

Ah Kow objected. "What? I have to sit by the door all day and bark at people, and what do I get? Leftovers! This isn't right. I'll take 10 and you can have the remaining 10 years back!"

God nodded.

On the third day, God created the monkey. He said, "Mah Lau (monkey), your job is to entertain[5] people. You will make faces,

在中国，上帝最初创造了牛。他对牛说："牛啊，你的工作就是整天和农夫一起去地里干活。你有力气拉东西，你还要产奶给人喝。你将整天在太阳底下干活，你的回报就是你只能吃草。因为那样，你可以活50年。"

牛不同意。"什么？我整天在太阳底下干活，却只能吃草？除此之外，居然还要把我的奶给别人喝。那么辛苦，还要我活50年，我只要20年就够了，剩下的30年你收回去吧。"

上帝同意了。

第二天，上帝创造了狗，他说："狗啊，我是有目的才造你的。你必须整天坐在你主人的门口，如果有人来，你就要冲他叫。因为那样，你可以吃你主人剩下的饭菜。给你20年的生命吧。"

狗也不同意。"我整天坐在门口朝人叫喊，我得到了什么？剩菜剩饭！这不公平，我只要活10年，那10年你收回去吧。"

上帝点了点头。

第三天上帝创造了猴子，他说："猴啊，你的工作是给人们提供娱乐，你做鬼脸，行为滑稽，让人们笑。你还可以翻跟头，在树上摇荡来逗他们开心。你呢，会得到香蕉和

① **create**
/kriˈeɪt/
v. 创造
② **energy**
/ˈenədʒɪ/
n. 能量，力气
③ **in turn**
回报
④ **object**
/ˈɒbdʒɪkt/
v. 反对
⑤ **entertain**
/ˌentəˈteɪn/
v. 娱乐

act stupid and make them laugh. You will also do somersaults[6] and swing[7] on trees to amuse them. In return, you will get to eat bananas and peanuts. For that, I'll give you 20 years to live."

Naturally the monkey objected. "This is ridiculous. I've got to make people laugh, do somersaults and even swing from tree to tree. What if I give you 10 years to say thanks for my existence[8] and just take 10?"

Again, God agreed.

On the fourth day, God created man and said to him, "You are my best piece of work. For that, you will only need to sleep, eat, play, eat, sleep again and do nothing else. You will get to eat all the best foods and play with the best toys. All you have to do is enjoy yourself. I'll give you 20 years of this kind of life."

Just like the other creations, man objected. "What? All I have to do is relax and enjoy myself and I only get 20 years? Tell you what: you have 30 years back from Ah Ngau, 10 from Ah Kow and another 10 from Mah Lau. You probably don't know what to do with all those years. Why don't I take them all, then I'll have 70 years to live?"

God, being good-natured, agreed with a smile. And that is why now ...

花生吃。我给你 20 年的生命吧。"

当然猴子也不同意。"这太可笑了。我逗人们乐、翻跟头、在树上荡来荡去。我还是还给你 10 年吧，就算是谢谢你让我来到这个世界上，我只要活 10 年。"

上帝又同意了。

第四天上帝创造了人，他对人说："你是我最出色的杰作。你只需要睡觉、吃饭、玩耍，再吃饭、再睡觉，什么都不需要做。你可以吃最好的食物，玩最好的玩具，你要做的只是享乐。我给你 20 年过这样的生活。"

像其他动物一样，人也不同意。"什么？我要做的只是玩耍、享乐，而我却只能活 20 年？跟你说吧，你从牛那收回了 30 年，从狗那收回了 10 年，从猴子那收回了 10 年，你大概不知道怎么安排吧，为什么不给我呢？那样我就可以活 70 年了。"

上帝好心，笑着同意了，这就是为什么：

我们头 20 年吃、睡、玩、享乐，接下来的 30 年为了养家像牛一样工作，再接下

❻ **somersault**
/ˈsʌməsɔːlt/
n. 翻跟头
❼ **swing** /swɪŋ/
v. 荡来荡去
❽ **existence**
/ɪɡˈzɪstəns/
n. 存在

We eat, sleep, play and enjoy ourselves in the first 20 years of our life, work like a cow for the next 30 to raise our family, then sit outside the door and bark at people for the next 10, after retirement[9]. Finally, we make faces and perform monkey tricks to entertain our grandchildren in the last 10 years of our life.

来 10 年，退休后像狗一样坐在门口冲人叫
嚷，生命中最后的 10 年我们做鬼脸、扮猴相
逗孙子乐。

❾ retirement
/rɪˈtaɪəmənt/
n. 退休

The bully
坏 小 子

As how I feel in this wheelchair is just like how you felt way back then when you lived in the orphan home.

我坐在轮椅上的感受和你当时在孤儿院的感受一样。

I walked into the Huddle House restaurant in Brunswick, Georgia, and sat down at the counter[1] as all of the booths[2] were taken. I picked up a menu and began to look at the various items, trying to decide if I wanted to order breakfast or just go ahead and eat lunch.

"Excuse me", said someone, as she touched me on the shoulder.

I looked up and turned to the side to see a rather nice-looking woman standing before me.

"Is your name Roger by any chance?" She asked.
"Yes," I responded, looking rather confused, as I had never seen her before.

"My name is Barbara and my husband is Tony," she said, pointing to a distant table near the door leading into the bathrooms.

I looked where she was pointing but did not recognize the man sitting alone at the table.

"I'm sorry ... I don't think I know you guys. But my name is Roger. Roger Kiser," I told her.

"Tony Claxton. Tony from Landon High School in Jacksonville, Florida?" She asked me.
"I'm really sorry. The name doesn't <u>ring a bell[3]</u>".

She turned, walked back to her table and sat down. She and

我走进佐治亚州布伦维尔区的"会友轩"餐馆，由于所有的包间都已客满，我就坐在了柜台旁。我拿起菜单，边看各种各样的菜名，边决定我应该点早餐还是直接吃午餐。

　　"对不起。"有人拍拍我的肩膀说。

　　我转过身去，抬头看到一个非常漂亮的妇女站在我面前。

　　"你是罗杰吗？"她问。

　　"是的。"我回答道，我很纳闷，因为我以前从来没见过她。

　　"我叫芭芭拉，我丈夫叫托尼。"她指着远处通向洗手间的门旁边的一张桌子说。

　　我顺着她指的方向看去，但是没认出独自坐在桌子旁边的那个人。

　　"对不起……我想我不认识你们。我的名字是罗杰。罗杰·凯塞。"我告诉她说。

　　"托尼·克拉克斯顿。佛罗里达州雅克维尔区伦敦高中的托尼，你不认识吗？"她问我。

　　"真是对不起，这个名字听起来不耳熟。"

　　她转身回到她的桌旁坐下，然后和她丈夫开始交谈起来。过了一会儿，我看到她坐在位子上转过身来，盯着我看。

❶ counter
/ˈkaʊntə(r)/
n. 柜台
❷ booth /buːθ/
n. 小房间
❸ ring a bell
听起来耳熟

her husband immediately began talking and once in a while, I would see her turn around in her seat and look directly at me.

I finally decided to order breakfast and a cup of decaffeinated[4] coffee. I sat there racking[5] my brain, trying to remember who this Tony was.

I must know him, I thought to myself. He recognizes me for some reason. I picked up my coffee up and took a sip. All of a sudden it came to me like a flash of lighting.

Tony. TONY THE BULLY? I mumbled[6], as I swung around[7] on my stool and faced his direction. The bully of my seventh grade Geography class?

How many times had that sorry guy made fun of my big ears in front of the girls in class? How many times had this sorry son-of-a-gun laughed at me because I had no parents and had to live in an orphanage? How many times had this big bully slammed[8] me up against the lockers[9] in the hallway just to make himself look like a big man to all the other students?

He raised his hand and waved. I smiled, returned the wave, turned back and began to eat my breakfast.

Jesus. He's so thin now. Not the big burly[10] guy I remember from back in 1957, I thought to myself.

All of a sudden I heard the sound of dishes breaking, so I

我最终决定点一份早餐和一杯不含咖啡因的咖啡。我坐在那绞尽脑汁，想这个托尼是谁。

我一定认识他，我自言自语。因为某种原因，他认出了我。我端起咖啡杯喝了一口，突然像有一道闪电闪过，我想起来了。

托尼，托尼是那个坏小子吗？我嘀咕着，突然转过身朝着他的方向望去。我七年级地理班上的那个小坏蛋？

好多次这个坏小子在班上女生面前取笑我的大耳朵，好多次这个可恶的小子因为我没有父母，不得不生活在孤儿院而嘲笑我，好多次这个大混小子把我撞在门厅的橱柜上，仅仅是为了在其他同学面前显露他像个男子汉。

他抬起手挥了挥，我笑了笑，也朝他挥了挥手，转回身来开始吃我的早餐。

上帝！他现在太瘦了，不是我记得的1957年时候的那个强壮的小伙子了。我对自己说。

突然我听到盘子打碎的声音，于是我马上转过身去看发生了什么事。原来，托尼和他的妻子吃饭时把他的轮椅停在了通往洗手间的走廊里，托尼想坐到轮椅上时，碰掉了桌上的几个盘子。服务生跑过来开始捡地上

❹ decaffeinated
/diˈkæfɪneɪtɪd/
adj. 除去咖啡因的

❺ rack /ræk/
v. 绞尽脑汁

❻ mumble
/ˈmʌmbl/
v. 嘀咕

❼ swing around
突然转向相反方向

❽ slam
/slæm/
v. 猛击

❾ locker
/ˈlɒkə(r)/
n. 小橱柜

❿ burly /ˈbɜːlɪ/
adj. 结实，强壮的

spun around to see what had happened. Tony had knocked several plates off the table as he tried to get into his wheelchair, which had been parked in the bathroom hallway while they were eating. The waitress ran over and started picking up the broken dishes and I listened as Tony and his wife tried to apologize.

As Tony rolled by me, pushed by his wife, I looked up and I smiled.

"Roger," he said, as he nodded.
"Tony," I responded, nodding my head in return.

I watched as they went out of the door and slowly made their way to a large van[11] which had a wheelchair loader located on its side door.

I sat and watched as his wife tried, again and again, to get the ramp[12] to come down. But it just would not work. Finally I got up, paid for my meal, and walked up to the van.

"What's the problem?"
"Darn[13] thing sticks once in a while," said Tony.
"Would you help me get him in the van?" Asked his wife.
"I think I can do that," I said, as I grabbed the wheelchair and rolled Tony over to the passenger door.

I opened the door and locked the brakes[14] on the wheelchair.

"Okay. Arms around the neck, Dude," I said as I reached

的碎片。我听到托尼和他的妻子的道歉声。

托尼坐在轮椅上，由妻子推着经过我的身边。他看到我，身子晃动起来，我抬眼看了一下，笑了。

"罗杰。"他边说边点头。

"托尼。"我也点头说。

我目送着他们走出门，慢慢走向大货车，货车的门旁边有可以装轮椅的地方。

我坐下来看他的妻子想把斜板弄下来，但她试了一次又一次都不行。最后我站起来，付了钱，走向大货车。

"怎么了?"

"老是被烦人的东西粘住。"托尼说。

"你能帮我把他抬进货车吗?"他妻子问。

"可以。"我说。我抓住轮椅，把托尼推到门边。

我打开门，把轮椅的闸挂上。

"好，用胳膊抱住我的脖子，老兄。"说着我俯下身抱住他的腰，小心地把他放到副驾驶座上。

托尼的胳膊松开了，我伸过手把他麻木的无知觉的腿挪进车里，放在他前面。

"你记得，是吗?"他直视着我的眼睛说。

"是的，托尼。"

⓫ **van** /væn/
n. 货车
⓬ **ramp** /ræmp/
n. 斜坡，斜面
⓭ **darn** /dɑːn/
adj. 烦人的
⓮ **brake** /breɪk/
n. 闸

down, grabbed him around the waist and carefully raised him up onto the passenger seat.

As Tony let go of my neck, I reached over and swung his limp, lifeless legs, one at a time, into the van so that they could be stationed directly in front of him.

"You remember, don't you?" He said, looking into my eyes.

"I remember, Tony?"

"I guess you're thinking, what goes around comes around?" He said, softly.

"I would never think like that, Tony," I said, with a stern[15] look on my face.

He reached over, grabbed both my hands and squeezed them tightly.

"As how I feel in this wheelchair is just like how you felt way back then when you lived in the orphan home."

"Almost, Tony. You are very lucky. You have someone to push you around who loves you. I didn't have anyone."

I reached in my pocket, pulled out one of my cards and handed it to him. "Give me a call. We'll do lunch."

We both laughed. I stood there watching as they drove toward the interstate[16] and finally disappeared onto the southbound[17] ramp. I hope he calls me sometime. He will be the only friend I have from my high school days.

"我猜你在想，这是报应！"他轻声说道。

"我从来没那样想过，托尼。"我说，脸显得很严肃。

他伸过手来抓住了我的双手，紧紧地握着。

"我坐在轮椅上的感受和你当时在孤儿院的感受一样。"

"差不多吧，托尼。但是你是幸运的，你有爱你的人推你四处走走，当时我身边却一个人都没有。"

我把手伸进口袋，掏出一张名片递给他，"给我打电话，我们一起吃顿午饭。"

我们都笑了。我站在那儿看他们向另一个州驶去，最后消失在南行的斜坡上。我希望某个时候他给我打电话。他将是我惟一的高中时代的朋友。

⑮ stern /stɜːn/
adj. 严肃的
⑯ interstate
/'ɪntəsteɪt/
n. 州际公路
⑰ southbound
/'saʊθbaʊnd/
adj. 南行的

The miser[1]

守财奴

So there must be some good reason for the old man to take all the insults all these years!

所以这些年，这个老人忍受所有的侮辱一定有他自己的理由。

A crowd of people was running through one of the main streets of Mexico, hooting[2] and shrieking[3] at an old man who tried to get away from them. Pelted[4] as he was, and hunted like a wild beast, the poor old man seemed to have no malice[5] against them.

As the streets were not built on even ground with potholes[6] in-between, the old man had to hobble[7] down one street and up another. His pursuers seemed to enjoy the chase and called him insulting names. No one made any attempt to help him or to restrain the crowd. Shopkeepers[8] stood at their front doors, old men and women sat by the wayside and remained perfectly indifferent to the scene in front of them.

A group of tourists happened to pass by. Many too just shook their heads and continued on their journey. But one tourist who was curious went up to one of the shopkeepers and asked why they were chasing the old man.

"Oh, he's a wicked[9] old man who never did good to anyone, and the people always chased him like this." A customer who was standing by, added, "he ought to be used to it now, for he has had to put up with it for ten years at least. Serve him right[10] too!"

A dialogue soon emerged between the tourist and the shopkeeper with more people cheeping[11] in their opinion.

"But has he injured anyone?"

一群人跑着穿过墨西哥的一条主街，朝一个试图远离他们的老人尖叫。尽管这个可怜的老人被攻击，像一个野兽一样被追赶，可他似乎对他们没有任何敌意。

这些街道并不平坦，到处都坑坑洼洼的，老人只好步履蹒跚地从一个街道跑到另一个街道。追赶他的人们似乎很喜欢追他，还骂他。没有一个人想帮他或阻止人群。店主站在前门口，老人和妇女坐在路边，对眼前发生的事情袖手旁观。

一群游客正好路过，很多人也只是摇摇头，继续前行。但是有一个好奇的游客走上前去问一个店主，为什么他们要追赶老人。

"哦，他是个恶毒的老头，从来不做好事，人们经常像这样追赶他。"一个站在旁边的顾客说，"现在他应该习惯了，因为他已经忍受至少10年了。他真是活该！"

这个游客就和店主谈起来了，越来越多的人也唧唧喳喳地说出了他们的观点。

"他伤害过任何人吗？"

"没有，他太虚弱，伤不了别人。"

"那么为什么他们要侮辱他呢？"

"仅仅是因为他是一个守财奴，他攒了好多钱，但即使是为自己，他也舍不得花一

❶ miser /ˈmaɪzə(r)/ n. 守财奴
❷ hoot /huːt/ v. 叫喊
❸ shriek /ʃriːk/ v. 尖叫
❹ pelt /pelt/ v. 投掷
❺ malice /ˈmælɪs/ n. 怨恨，敌意
❻ pothole /ˈpɒthəʊl/ n. 坑洼
❼ hobble /ˈhɒbl/ v. 跛行，蹒跚
❽ shopkeeper /ˈʃɒpkiːpə(r)/ n. 店主，零售商
❾ wicked /ˈwɪkɪd/ adj. 邪恶的
❿ serve sb right 活该
⓫ cheep /tʃiːp/ v. 唧唧喳喳地叫

"Oh no, he is too feeble[12] for that."

"Then why do they insult him?"

"Simply because he is a miser. He hoards[13] his money and never spends a single dime[14] more than he can help, even on himself."

"All I can tell is what I gathered from my late father. The old man worked on board a ship. I am not sure if it was an American or a British ship or whether he was a captain or an ordinary sailor. Unlike most sailors with a wife or mistress at every port, this old man never got married. So you can imagine how much money he must have saved. Why he chose to retire in our city, this, I cannot tell you. But he is certainly not one of our locals."

"Do you know his name and where he stays?"

"I'm only a shopkeeper and all I know may be hearsay[15]. If you're really interested there is someone who can solve your mystery. He's what we call a busybody[16] who makes it his duty to know all the goings-on in and around the city. If you can wait a little longer, the busybody will soon be around. He always comes to my shop in the mornings on the look out for clients."

The tourist took out his card and handed it to the shopkeeper. "My name is Jack Robinson, a journalist and an Englishman. For a week I have been watching the same scene daily. People chase

个子儿。"

"这是我去世的父亲告诉我的。说是这个老人在船上工作。我不知道是美国船还是英国船，也不知道他是船长还是普通水手。每到一个港口，这个老人不像大多数水手去见妻子或找情人，他从来没有结婚，所以你可以想像他攒了多少钱。为什么退休后他选择我们这个城市，我不知道，但是他一定不是我们本地人。"

"你知道他的名字吗？他住哪儿？"

"我只是个卖货的，所知道的可能也只是道听途说。如果你真感兴趣，有一个人可以为你解开谜团。他是一个好管闲事的人，打听城里城外发生的事情是他的职责。你等一会儿，他马上就要来了，他总是早上到我店里来兜揽生意。"

游客拿出一张名片递给店主。"我叫杰克·鲁滨逊，是个英国记者。这一星期我每天都在观察着这一情景，人们追赶这位老人，而老人却不说一句话。举个例子吧，假如你有一条狗，人们老追你的狗，它可能一天、两天甚至一个星期只是叫，不咬人。但肯定有一天你的狗会报复，伤害追赶它的人。所以，这些年，这个老人忍受所有的侮

⓬ **feeble** /ˈfiːbl/
adj. 虚弱的
⓭ **hoard** /hɔːd/
v. 储藏，积聚
⓮ **dime** /daɪm/
n. 美国，加拿大10分铸币
⓯ **hearsay**
/ˈhɪəseɪ/
n. 道听途说
⓰ **busybody**
/ˈbɪzɪbɒdɪ/
n. 好管闲事的人

the old man and he has not uttered a word. For instance, if you have a dog and people keep chasing after your dog, it might only bark but not bite for a day, two days or even a week. Surely some day your dog will retaliate[17] and do harm to his attackers! So there must be some good reason for the old man to take all the insults all these years! Why don't you people leave him alone?" Suddenly there was complete silence and no more words were heard. A cheerful looking man came in. It was the busybody and seeing the tensed situation said, "What's the matter with you people? Why the glum[18] sight faces?"

His eyes caught sight of the tourist. "Sir, can I help you? You want to sightsee[19], a special place, people, anything you want, and I'm at your service." With a giggle, he added, "just for a small ... fee, of course!"

"I'm interested to use your service. I want to find the old man ..." "Oh that silly old man! I know where he lives. But I'm not sure if he will open the door for you. But we can try! Let's go! It's somewhere in rather quiet back street away from this madding crowd."

To their luck as soon as they reached the house, the old man was just about to go in.

"Hi, sir, there's a visitor to see you," the busybody shouted. The old man turned but he did not give a second glance. Jack Robinson was quick to grasp the old man's hand.

辱一定有他自己的理由。人们为什么不放过他呢？"突然全场安静下来，没有一个人说话。一个满脸阳光的人进来了，是那个好事者。他看到这紧张的气氛说："你们怎么啦？为什么看起来闷闷不乐呢？"

他看到了那个游客，"先生，我能帮你吗？你想观光，想要看特别一点的地方、人还是其他什么。我可以做你的导游。"他咯咯地笑着，又说，"当然只要一点点钱。"

"我很高兴你能做我的向导，我想找到那个老人……"

"那个傻老头！我知道他住哪，但是我不确定他是否会为你开门，不过我们可以试一试，走吧！他住在非常僻静的后街的某个地方，远离这些疯狂的人群。"

很幸运，当他们到那的时候，那个老人正要进去。"你好，先生，这有一个游客要见你。"好事者嚷道。老人转过身来，但只瞥了一眼。杰克·鲁滨逊迅速拽住了老人的手。

"先生，请给我几分钟。我正在寻找一位失散多年的舅舅，我妈妈的弟弟。我答应她要不停地找他。我叫杰克……鲁滨逊是我的姓。你是不是我失散多年的舅舅？"

老人站在那儿不动，表情严肃。过了好

17 retaliate
/riˈtælɪeɪt/
v. 报复

18 glum /glʌm/
adj. 忧郁的

19 sightsee
/ˈsaɪtsɪ/
v. 观光，旅游

"Sir, give me a few minutes please. I'm looking for a long lost uncle, my mother's brother. She made me promise that I keep on looking for him. My name is Jack ... Robinson is the family name! Can you be my long lost uncle?"

The old man stood still and appeared solemn[20]. At long last, he replied. "After I came to stay here, I just changed my name to Robinson Crusoe. My real name is also Jack and Robinson is the family name. But I am not sure if I'm the man you are looking for. Anyway, I have an old photo of my sister and I taken in the orphanage before we got separated." He took out the snap[21] shot and showed it to Jack Robinson, the tourist.

From his coat pocket, Jack Robinson, the tourist, took out a small photo showing a small boy and a girl. "Do you recognize this photo?" He asked the old man. Tears fell down the old man's face, for the two photographs matched like <u>two peas in a pod</u>[22].

"Jack, there's no doubt your mother is my sister, Agnes. I have been thinking about her all these years," the old man cried. "You want to know why I did not retaliate when people kept chasing after me! Well, as an orphan boy I used to run away from one home to another whenever I was mistreated. But I never lost my English sense of humor, I needed exercise. It kept me <u>on my toes</u>[23]! I also never lost hope that my sister would be among the crowd of tourists to visit Mexico and she would somehow recognize me. It's like looking for a needle in a haystack[24] but I keep on hoping and praying."

长时间，他说："我来这以后就改名叫鲁滨逊·克鲁索。我真名也叫杰克，鲁滨逊是我的姓。我不知道我是不是你要找的人。不过我有一张我姐姐的照片，这是我们分开前在孤儿院照的。"他拿出照片递给杰克·鲁滨逊，那个游客。

杰克·鲁滨逊，那个游客，从他的上衣口袋里掏出一张小照片，上面是一个小男孩和一个小女孩。"你认得这张照片吗？"他问老人。老人看了之后眼泪顺着脸颊流下来，因为这两张照片是一模一样的。

"杰克，毫无疑问你妈妈是我姐姐，安吉。这些年我一直想着她。"老人哭着说，"你想知道人们追我时为什么我没有反抗吗？小时候是个孤儿，人们虐待我时，我经常从一家跑到另一家，但是我从没有丧失作为一个英国人的幽默感，我需要锻炼，这使我保持警觉。我也从没有放弃这样的希望：我姐姐可能就在来墨西哥旅游的游客之中，她可能会认出我。这犹如大海捞针，但我还是不停地希望、祈祷。"

"杰克舅舅，你是守财奴吗？镇上的人那么恨你。"

"不，杰克，他们并不恨我，因为他们

⑳ solemn
/'sɔləm/
adj. 严肃的
㉑ snap /snæp/
n. 照片
㉒ two peas in
a pod
一模一样
㉓ on one's toes
警觉的
㉔ haystack
/'heɪstæk/
n. 干草垛

"Are you a miser, uncle Jack that the town folks hate you so much?"

"No Jack, I don't think they hate me. It's because they have nothing much to do. I let them have their enjoyments, as there are more people than jobs here. I have saved and stinted[25] so that when I die all my investments, savings and even this house could be put to good use. But I am upset to see the young boys and girls who idle their lives away. They should be at school. Mexico is a heaven for retirees like me. Living is cheap and I love the people."

The busybody who was listening to the uncle and nephew conversation interrupted, "So that's why you did not say a word to your pursuers? What a joke!"

What a twist of fate that brought the old man to be united with his nephew, he never knew he had.

"Jack, will you bring your mother to visit me? In fact I would love to have her stay with me, at least for a while. "

"Uncle, mother now lives in Singapore. You see, father was sent to Singapore to work and after he died, mother decided to settle there. She loves its warm climate, and its way of life, spicy[26] hot food included. Father's widowed sister wanted mother to return to London and live with her but mother refused.

"Mother is very cosmopolitan[27] minded. She finds it fascinating

并没有其他事情可做。这里人多，工作少，我想让他们有更多的欢娱。我很节俭，为的就是当我死后，我的投资、储蓄，甚至这幢房屋都可以派上好用场。但是，我看到这些年轻的男孩女孩虚度光阴，我感到很难过。他们应该去上学，墨西哥是像我这样退休的老人的天堂。这里物价很低，而且我喜欢这里的人。"

一直听舅舅和外甥谈话的好事者插了一句："那就是你对你的追赶者不说一句话的原因？真是不可思议！"

曲折的命运使这个老人和外甥重逢。他从不知道会是这样。

"杰克，把你妈妈带来吧，事实上，我很想和她呆在一起，哪怕只是一小会儿。"

"叔叔，妈妈现在住在新加坡，你知道爸爸被派往新加坡工作，他死后妈妈就决定定居在那儿。她喜欢那里温暖的气候、生活方式，还有辛辣的食物。丧偶的姑姑想要妈妈回伦敦和她一起住，但是妈妈拒绝了。

妈妈具有世界性观念。她觉得中国人、印度人、马来西亚人、欧亚大陆人和其他民族的人在狮城新加坡混合在一起融洽地生活很有意思。

㉕ **stint** /stɪnt/
v. 节俭，限制
㉖ **spicy** /ˈspaɪsɪ/
adj. 香辣的
㉗ **cosmopolitan**
/ˌkɒzməˈpɒlɪtən/
adj. 世界性的，国际的

that the Chinese, Indians, Malays, Eurasians and many other nationalities mingling harmoniously together in Singapore called the Lion City.

"I vividly remember my engagement day to my Eurasian girl-friend, Eve whose father is American and mother is Chinese. Let me recollect what mother said to both of us: 'Eve, Jack, I would not like to contradict my famous countryman[28], Mark Twain who wrote: East is East and West is West and the twain shall never meet. He may have his reasons to pen his views and I have mine. Now to see my son Jack engaged to you, Eve, a Eurasian, gives me joy and a meaningful way of looking at life. East has mingled with the West and the twain did meet!' So uncle, mother would also be fascinated with Mexico. It was she kept the fire burning that one day she would be reunited with you."

"My sister is really open-minded who updates herself with the changing of the guards, as the English would say. I cannot wait to see her again. Let's phone her up and tell her the new news."

"Uncle, you're just as magnanimous[29] as mother. To keep up with the torments[30] for ten long years and yet you say, you love them."

The reunion of the old man and his nephew spread like wild fire. Jack Robinson, the young tourist had his story "The Miser" published. His uncle's house had non-stop visitors who came to apologize for what they had done to him. Even the mayor of the

我的女朋友伊夫是欧亚混血儿，我俩订婚的日子我还记忆犹新。伊夫的爸爸是个美国人，妈妈是个中国人。我还记得妈妈对我俩说:'伊夫，杰克，我并不是反对我著名的同胞马克·吐温的话，他说东方是东方，西方是西方，两者不能融合。他那样说有他的理由，我也有我的理由。现在看到我的儿子和你，伊夫，一个欧亚混血儿结婚，这给我带来欢乐，还给我一种更有意义的生活方式。东方和西方融合了，真的!' 所以舅舅，妈妈也会喜欢墨西哥的，她一直抱有这种信念，相信有一天会与你团聚的。"

　　"我姐姐真是开明，拿英国话来说，是跟得上形势。我等不及要见她了。给她打电话，告诉她这个最新消息吧。"

　　"舅舅，你和妈妈一样慷慨。你忍受他们 10 年的折磨，居然还说你爱他们。"

　　老人和外甥重逢的消息像野火一样传开了。杰克·鲁滨逊，年轻的游客出版了他的故事"守财奴"。舅舅的屋里不断地有访客来，为他们以前做过的事向他道歉，甚至镇长也来拜访他说:"我听说你的姐姐要来看你，她来的时候请告诉我，我将邀请城里的老老少少来欢聚一堂，更多地了解你。"

㉘ countryman
/ˈkʌntrɪmən/
n. 同胞
㉙ magnanimous
/mægˈnænɪməs/
adj. 慷慨的
㉚ torment
/ˈtɔːment/
n. 折磨

town came to pay the old man a visit and said, "I heard your sister is coming to visit you. Please let me know when she is here. I will then invite the town folks, young and old, and we will celebrate and get to know you better."

Moral: Life's journey is one of twists and turns. Here "patience" is the keyword.

　　寓意：生活的道路曲曲折折，"耐心"
是最重要的。

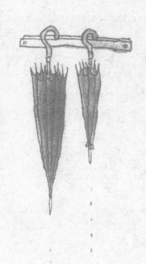

The potter

陶　工

There were times when I wanted to call it quits because I wasn't sure if this road I had taken was worth it.

很多次我都想放弃，因为我不清楚这条路是否值得走下去。

We often set sail into the great big world with high expectations. If you're lucky, you will return with a smile on your face, and perhaps a nice tan[1] to complement the riches you have accumulated. If not, well ... I wish I knew then what I know now. Then, perhaps, I wouldn't have wasted all those years.

It was almost a decade ago, and I had just finished college. With my degree in hand, and a truckload of ego[2] and confidence, I donned[3] slick[4] designed clothes to impress during my first interview.

The building where I had to go for the interview was one I hadn't heard of before. Feeling miffed[5] that the weather in my country shines kindly only upon cotton and loose clothing, I wished I could have stayed on in Australia. Then I wouldn't have to think twice about wearing thick (and expensive!) suits.

As I furiously[6] wiped the sweat off my sticky face, I came to an old building. It looked run-down and neglected.

I looked around for an air-conditioned partition, an office maybe. However, all I saw was a huge collection of ceramic[7] pots, and a man sitting amidst the clutter[8].

The slight, sun burnt person smiled and squinted[9] his eyes. He stopped work to look at me.

As I approached him and showed him the paper with the address of the building I wanted, he didn't budge[10] at all. But he blinked[11] once or twice because of the glaring sun. And that smile

我们经常带着很高的期望启航环游大千世界。如果幸运的话，回来时脸上笑容满面，可能在你积累的丰富经历之外还晒得一身健美的皮肤。如果不幸运，那么……要是那时我知道我现在知道的就好了，可能我就不会浪费那些年了。

大约是 10 年前，我刚刚读完大学。因为我有学历，所以非常自负和自信。为了使我第一次面试留下好印象，我穿上了订做的质地光滑的衣服。

我前去面试的那座大楼我以前从来没听说过。在我国，太阳只会和善地对待身穿宽松的棉质衣服的人，这一点让我很气愤，我希望我能呆在澳大利亚，那样我就不用再三考虑是否穿厚厚的（而且昂贵的）西装了。

当我正满腔愤怒地把汗从我粘糊糊的脸上擦去时，我来到一幢旧楼前，它看起来很破旧，不显眼。

我看看四周，想找一个有空调的地方，比如说一间办公室。然而，我所看到的都是大堆的陶器，还看到一个人坐在凌乱的东西之间。

这个瘦弱的、被太阳晒伤的人眯着眼冲我笑。他停下工作看着我。

我走近他，把写着我想要找的地址的纸

❶ tan /tæn/
n. 皮肤晒黑

❷ ego /ˈiːgəu/
n. 自负

❸ don /dɒn/
v. 穿

❹ slick /slɪk/
adj. 光滑的

❺ miff /mɪf/
v. 生气，发怒

❻ furiously
/ˈfjʊərɪəslɪ/
adv. 满腔愤怒的

❼ ceramic
/sɪˈræmɪk/
adj. 陶器的

❽ clutter
/ˈklʌtə(r)/
n. 凌乱的东西

stayed on his face.

"Do you know where this is?" I asked rather importantly, like I was late for a crucial meeting.

He looked at the paper, then at me, and his smile grew wider.

"So, where is it? Do you know or not?" I was getting impatient.

"Not here," he replied.

"Uh?" I was almost speechless. All my time wasted, and my best clothes ... only to encounter this small person.

"Where's your boss?" I asked, hoping that he'd show me to a shiny flashy block behind the stack of ceramics.

"No boss. Everybody here helps make and sell our pots. We are looking for someone to meet and speak to our distributors[12]. You want the job?" Asked the man, who turned out to be the owner of the ceramics center.

With one eyebrow raised, I turned and didn't look back. I was angry with him for not being specific in the classified ads. I was angry, too, that the weather was so hot.

Later that week, I found my stylish[13] job at a multinational firm and was happy. But after a few weeks, I felt that the new friends I made there didn't really care for much except themselves and their work. After a few months, I realized, too, that I didn't care

给他看。他一动也没动，但是因为阳光太强，他眨了两下眼。他的脸上始终保持着微笑。

"你知道这地方在哪吗？"我趾高气扬地问道，就像一次重要的会议我迟到了。

他看看这张纸，又看了看我，笑得更灿烂了。

"在哪？你到底知不知道？"我不耐烦了。

"不在这。"他说。

"什么？"我几乎无话可说。我的时间都浪费了，还有我最好的衣服……结果却遇到了这么个不起眼的人。

"你们老板在哪？"我问，希望他从这堆陶器后面给我指一条路，通往耀眼繁华的街区。

"没有老板，这里的每一个人都帮忙做陶壶，卖陶壶。我们正在寻找一个人来和我们的批发商谈判。你想做这份工作吗？"那人问道，俨然成了这个陶器中心的主人。

我扬起一只眉毛，转过身去，再也没有往回看。我很生气，他在分类广告上没有说清楚具体做什么工作，而且天气还这么热。

那个周末，我在一家跨国公司找了一份体面的工作，我很高兴。但是几周过后，我

for much except my high-paying job and myself.

Yes, the money was good, but everything I earned was used to finance what I had bought the month before. And no matter how much more I earned, there was always something new to buy; something interesting to make my job worth it; something to boast about so my life would mean something; something to keep me happy for a few days at least.

The months soon turned into years, years filled with jealousy, hatred, backstabbing[14] and that unquenchable[15] hunger for more. There were times when I wanted to call it quits because I wasn't sure if this road I had taken was worth it.

Then, last month, I was assigned to return to my hometown to meet a new client. The address looked familiar.

On my way there, my suspicions were confirmed: I would be dealing with the ceramics boss. I quickly figured a way to handle things smoothly. I would pretend that I'd never met him before.

I felt at ease again as I walked in and saw him, crouched[16] over some pots, his hands caked with clay[17].

It was hot, the ceramic pots were still piled up high, and that same smile shone brightly under the afternoon sun. Nothing had changed.

I introduced myself, and flashed my fake smile before proceeding to the documents. As I opened my briefcase, I noticed the small man looking at me. I looked up and saw him smiling like a fool.

感觉我在那儿交的新朋友除了他们自己和工作之外并不真正关心其他的事情。几个月后，我还发现除了薪水高的工作和我自己外，我也对其他不在乎。

是的，有钱真好，但我所挣的只是为了支付上个月买的东西。不管我挣多少，总有新东西要买。其中一些有趣的东西是为了使我觉得这个工作还值得去做，一些东西是为了炫耀，这样我的生活才有点意义，一些东西为的是至少让我高兴几天。

月复一月，年复一年，生活中总是充满嫉妒、仇恨，我总是感到腹背受敌，欲望越来越多。很多次我都想放弃，因为我不清楚这条路是否值得走下去。

上个月，我被派回我的故乡去见一个新客户，地址看起来很熟悉。

到那儿后，我的怀疑被证实了：我将会和陶器厂老板谈判。我很快想出了一个让事情顺利进行的办法，那就是假装以前没有遇到过他。

我很坦然地走过去，看着他。他蹲在一些陶壶中间，手上粘满了黏土。

天气很热。陶壶仍堆得很高，同样的笑容在午后的阳光下显得很耀眼。什么也没改变。

⑬ **stylish**
/'staɪlɪʃ/
adj. 体面的

⑭ **backstab**
/'bækstæb/
v. 腹背受敌

⑮ **unquenchable**
/ʌn'kwentʃəbl/
adj. 不可扑灭的

⑯ **crouch**
/'kraʊtʃ/
v. 蹲

⑰ **clay** /kleɪ/
n. 黏土

I forgot that he was a client and blurted[18], "What? Why are you always smiling?"

I felt a horrible sense of regret. Yet, there was relief for it had been a long time since I last lashed out in frustration.

"I've almost finished with this piece. See. This bowl was first gathered from the ground, wet, and then kneaded[19] to perfection. I spent hours shaping it and removing the imperfections so that it would be beautiful.

"After that, I burnt it in the kiln[20], watching it closely to ensure the temperature was not too hot. Then I left it to cool, and waited until I could continue working on it again. When it is ready, I will stroke its comforting crimson[21] body with the glorious colors of the rainbow."

When he finished talking, the man held up the ceramic pot. I took it from him for a closer look. Yes, even though it wasn't quite finished, the pot looked beautiful.

"Be careful. If it drops, all that's left will be the broken pieces. If you glue it back, it will never be the same again. But you can still change its appearance. All you need is some paint, and some more time. Do you mind waiting for me while I finish?" The man asked.

I looked at him, smiled, and nodded my head.

我作了一下自我介绍，在拿出文件之前挤出一丝微笑。当我打开手提箱的时候，我注意到那个矮小的人在看着我。我抬头看见他笑得像个傻子似的。

我忘记了他是我的客户，脱口说了一句："你为什么老是笑?"

我突然间有一种后悔的恐惧感。然而，这是一种长期遭受痛苦沮丧后的发泄。

"这件我基本上做好了，你看，做这只碗最先要从地上采土，湿土，然后捏成形。我花了几个小时塑造它，把不完美的地方弄得漂亮些。

"然后，把它放到窑里烧，密切注意，控制好温度，不要太高。然后让它自己冷却，等一会儿再继续做。一切就绪后，我再在这深红的成品上镶上彩虹般绚丽的颜色。"

他说完之后，举起陶壶。我从他手里拿过来仔细看了看。是的，即使它还没有完全做好，但看起来已经很漂亮了。

"小心点，如果它掉下来会摔成碎片的。用胶水粘住也不会像以前一样了，但是你还是可以改变它的外表。你所需要的只是一些涂料和时间。你介意等我把它做完吗?"那人问道。

我看着他，笑了，点了点头。

18 **blurt** /blɜːt/
v. 脱头口而出
19 **knead** /niːd/
v. 揉，搓
20 **kiln** /kɪln/
n. 窑
21 **crimson** /ˈkrɪmzn/
adj. 深红的，绯红的

The time account

时间账户

Well, each of us has such an account. Its name is TIME.

每个人都有这样一个账户，账户名是时间。

Say there is a bank that credits[1] your account[2] each morning with RMB86,400. Every evening, the bank deletes[3] whatever remains of this sum that you have failed to use during the day. It does not carry over[4] any balance from day to day.

What would you do if you had such an account?

Draw out every cent, every day, of course!

Well, each of us has such an account. Its name is TIME.

Every morning, Time credits you with 86,400 seconds. Every night it writes off[5], as lost, whatever you have failed to put to use. It carries over no balance. It allows no overdraft[6].

Each day, Time opens a new account for you. Each night, it burns whatever remains in the account. If you fail to use up all of the day's deposits, you can't keep them for tomorrow. Neither can you draw from what will be put in the next morning.

Time's clock runs non-stop.

To realize the value of one year, ask the student who has failed a grade.

To realize the value of one month, ask the mother who has given birth to a premature[7] baby.

假设有一家银行，每天早上往你的账户存入 86,400 元人民币，每天晚上，删除你当天没有用完的钱，而不会将账目转入下一天。

如果你有这么一个账户你会怎么做？

当然是每天取出所有的钱。

每个人都有这样一个账户，账户名是时间。

每天早上，时间给你存入 86,400 秒，每晚取消你没有利用的时间，不会自动转入第二天，也不允许透支。

每一天，时间为你开办一个新账户，每天晚上，把账户里所有剩下的都取消，就像丢了一样。如果你没有用完当天的储存你也不能保存到明天，也不能动用第二天的储蓄。

时钟在不停地奔跑。

要体会到一年的价值，就去问一个留级的学生。

要体会到一个月的价值，就去问一个早产的母亲。

要体会到一个星期的价值，就去问一个周报的编辑。

要体会到一个小时的价值，就去问一对等待见面的情人。

要体会到一分钟的价值，就去问一个刚

❶ credit
/ˈkredɪt/
v. 存款

❷ account
/əˈkaʊnt/
n. 账户

❸ delete
/dɪˈliːt/
v. 删除

❹ carry over
将账目转入下一页

❺ write off
取消

❻ overdraft
/ˈəʊvədrɑːft/
n. 透支

❼ premature
/ˈpremətjʊə(r)/
adj. 早产的

To realize the value of one week, ask the editor of a weekly newspaper.

To realize the value of one hour, ask two lovers who are waiting to meet.

To realize the value of one minute, ask the traveler who has just missed his train.

To realize the value of one second, ask the motorist who has just avoided an accident.

To realize the value of one millisecond[8], ask the athlete who has won a silver medal in the Olympics.

Treasure every moment that you have! And treasure it more because you have shared it with someone special, special enough to spend your time with. And remember that time waits for no one. Yesterday is history. Tomorrow is a mystery. Today is a gift. That's why it's called the present!

刚误了火车的旅行者。

　　要体会到一秒钟的价值，就去问一个刚刚躲过了一次事故的司机。

　　要体会到千分之一秒的价值，就去问一个刚在奥林匹克运动会上获得银牌的运动员。

　　珍惜你所拥有的每一秒钟，更加珍惜你和一个非常特别的人一起度过的时光。记住，时间不等人，昨天是历史，明天是未知，今天是礼物。这就是为什么在英语里"礼物"也它被称作"现在"的原因。

❽ **millisecond**

/ˈmɪlɪˌsekənd/

n. 千分之一秒

I wish you enough
知足常乐,尽享人生

Have you ever said goodbye to someone knowing that it would be forever?

你曾经明知是永别却还对他说再见吗?

At an airport I overheard[1] a father and daughter during their last moments together. Her flight was ready for boarding and they were standing near the departure[2] gate. She said, "Daddy, our life together has been more than enough. Your love is all I ever need. I wish you enough, too, Daddy. "

They kissed goodbye and she left. The man walked over towards the window near where I was seated. I could see that he wanted and needed to cry.

I tried not to intrude[3] upon his privacy, but he welcomed me by asking, "Have you ever said goodbye to someone knowing that it would be forever?"

"Yes, I have." Saying that brought back memories I had of expressing my love and appreciation[4] for all that my Dad had done for me. Recognizing that his days were numbered, I took the time to tell him, face-to-face, how much he meant to me. So I knew what this man was going through.

"Forgive me for asking, but why is this goodbye forever?" I asked.

"I am old and she lives much too far away. I have challenges ahead and the reality is, her next trip back will be for my funeral," he said.

"I heard you say, 'I wish you enough?' May I ask what that

在机场我无意中听到父女俩在最后分别时刻的谈话。女儿正准备上飞机，他们站在飞机门附近。女儿说："爸爸，我们在一起生活这么长时间我已经很知足了，你给我的爱也够了，我也希望你能知足常乐，尽享人生，爸爸！"

吻别后，女儿走了。父亲朝着我座位附近的窗子走过来，我可以看出他忍不住要哭。

我尽力不触及他的隐私，但他却向我打招呼，问："你曾经明知是永别却还对他说再见吗？"

"我有过这种经历。"这句话让我想起我曾为父亲为我所做的一切向他表示过我的爱和感激。知道他在世的日子不多后，我特意当面对他说他对我有多么重要。所以我理解这个人此时的感受。

"请原谅我问一句，为什么是永别呢？"我问。

"我老了，她又住得那么远。我的未来生活充满挑战。实际上，她再回来时是要参加我的葬礼了。"他说。

"我听到你说'我希望你知足常乐，尽享人生'。那是什么意思？"

他露出微笑。"那个愿望是我们家代代

❶ overhear
/ˌəʊvəˈhɪə(r)/
v. 无意中听到
❷ departure
/dɪˈpɑːtʃə(r)/
n. 分开，分离
❸ intrude
/ɪnˈtruːd/
v. 闯入，打搅
❹ appreciation
/əˌpriːʃɪˈeɪʃn/
n. 感谢

means?"

He began to smile. "That is a wish that has been <u>handed down</u>[5] through the generations. My parents used to say it to everyone. "

The man paused a moment, then looked up, as if trying to remember the details.

"Then we say I wish you enough. We want the other persons to have a life filled with enough good things to sustain[6] them."

He then turned me and shared the following, as if he were reciting[7] it from memory:

I wish you enough sun to keep your attitude[8] bright.
I wish you enough rain to appreciate the sun more.
I wish you enough happiness to keep your spirits up.
I wish you enough pain so that the smallest joys in life appear
    much bigger.
I wish you enough gain to satisfy your wanting.
I wish you enough loss to appreciate all that you possess.
I wish enough hellos to get you through the final Goodbye.

The man then began to sob and walked away.

相传的。我的父母过去常对每个人说。"那人
停顿了一下，抬了抬头，像是在尽力回想其
中的细节。

"我们对人们说知足常乐，尽享人生，
就是希望其对方的生活里充满幸事，支撑他
们走下去。"

他转向我，对我说了下面这些话，像是
在背诵：

我希望你有足够的阳光让你乐观

我希望你有足够的雨水让你更加感激阳
　　光

我希望你有足够的幸福使你情绪激昂

我希望你有足够的痛苦感受生命中微小
　　的欢乐带来的幸福

我希望你得到更多，满足你的需要

我希望你失去更多，珍惜所有

我希望在永别后能广交朋友

那个人开始抽噎，然后走开了。

⑤ **hand down**
代代相传
⑥ **sustain**
/səsˈteɪn/
v. 支撑
⑦ **recite** /rɪˈsaɪt/
v. 背诵
⑧ **attitude**
/ˈætɪtjuːd/
n. 态度

The boy who sang his blues away
唱走悲伤的男孩

Sing your blues away and make believe that everything will be alright.

唱走悲伤，相信一切都会好起来的。

Blue's father called out to him before he left home to find work in the town. "Son, remember what I told you. Take care of yourself. I'll be home as fast as I can."

Every morning after his father left, Blue would take a look at the blue coat his mother stitched[1] for him when he was a baby. It used to keep him warm but he had outgrown the coat. It was the most precious[2] gift from his mother. Though life was hard for father and son, Blue was always happy. "Sing your blues away, son," his father told him. His father preferred[2] the word "blues" instead of "troubles." "It sounds nicer, father," Blue replied. "You've grown into a big clever boy!" as father and son hugged each other.

"Son, these were the words your mother whispered[4] to me before she took her last breath, 'Husband, do you remember how we loved to walk and made our wishes, under the blue sky, as we went along? So I stitched a blue coat for our baby. Can you help me to put it on him?' Your mother then held you in her arms and continued softly, 'Our baby looks so pretty in the blue coat. Tell him I love him and I will watch over him wherever he goes. You're a good and brave husband. Teach our son to be like you.' 'Wife, I surely will! Shall we call our son Blue?' She was too weak to talk further and nodded her head lightly and gave a sweet smile. She died still holding you in her arms."

People usually sing when they are happy with plenty to eat but that was not the case for Blue. To start with, it was cold and there

布鲁的爸爸在离开家去城里找工作之前对布鲁说："儿子，记住我所说的话，照顾好自己，我会尽快回来的。"

爸爸走后，他每天早上都要看一看妈妈在他小时候为他缝的一件蓝上衣。以前是为了保暖，现在已经不能穿了。这是妈妈给他的最珍贵的礼物。尽管父子生活艰辛，布鲁总是很高兴。"把悲伤唱走，儿子。"爸爸告诉他。爸爸宁愿用"悲伤"，而不用"麻烦"。"这个词听起来更好一些，爸爸。"布鲁说。"你是一个聪明的大男孩了。"父子俩拥抱在一起。

"儿子，你妈妈在临终前轻声对我说：'你还记得我们多么喜欢在蓝天下散步，边走边许愿吗？所以我缝制了一件蓝上衣给我们的孩子。你帮我给他穿上吧。'你妈妈抱着你，继续说道：'我们的孩子穿蓝上衣真的很漂亮，告诉他我多么爱他，不管他到哪，我都会守护着他的。你是一个善良勇敢的丈夫，把我们的儿子也培养成像你一样的人吧。''我一定会的，我们给儿子取名叫巴路吧。'你妈妈太虚弱，说不出话了，只是轻轻点了点头，甜甜地笑了，她把你抱在怀里，静静地去了。"

通常，当人们能填饱肚子的时候，他们

❶ **stitch** /stɪtʃ/
v. 缝制
❷ **precious**
/'preʃəs/
adj. 珍贵的
❸ **prefer**
/prɪ'fɜː/
v. 更喜欢, 宁愿
❹ **whisper**
/'wɪspə(r)/
v. 低声说

were holes in his shoes. He had only a small bowl of rice porridge[5], his father had left him. Blue knew his father often went hungry but there was always a small bowl for him on the table. Blue kept himself busy, as he had to gather wood in the forest. He remembered his father's advice, "Sing your blues away and make believe that everything will be alright." So Blue sang and gathered his woods happily. As birds flew by, they too would chirp[6] along merrily when they heard Blue singing.

One day, he did not notice that a stranger was watching him. It was only when the man called out that Blue lifted up his head. "Boy, why are you singing? Are you not cold?" "I was but I've been so busy I am warm," replied Blue. "Your clothes are rags, you're thin and hungry. Surely you can't be happy. Why do you sing? It's silly." "Not at all, I had sung my blues away. I also convinced myself that I am the happiest boy in the country. I am really happy!"

"Oh, can you help me? I have a little boy who cries all day. I give him everything he asks for. Yet he is unhappy. Please come and sing him your song and teach him your secret. You're a brave little boy!" The stranger pleaded[7].

Blue nodded, "I will come after I have taken home the wood. When father comes home, there will be some wood to keep us warm. I go on singing until my heart opens up and sings too. I really have no secret."

就会很高兴地唱歌，但布鲁却不能。首先，天开始变冷了，他的鞋上还有洞。他只能吃爸爸留给他的一小碗稀饭。布鲁知道爸爸经常饿着肚子，但是桌上总会放着一小碗给他。布鲁每天很忙碌，因为他必须到森林里去捡柴。他记起爸爸的话："唱走悲伤，相信一切都会好起来的。"于是，布鲁边唱边高兴地捡柴。当有鸟飞过听到布鲁唱歌时，它们也欢快地唱起来。

一天，他没有注意到一个陌生人正注视着他，直到那个人叫他名字的时候，他才抬起头来。"孩子，你为什么唱歌啊？你不冷吗？""我冷啊，但是忙起来，我身子就暖和了。"布鲁答道。"你的衣服都破了，你又瘦又饿，一定不幸福，为什么唱歌呢？这多可笑。""一点也不可笑，我把悲伤唱走了。我还告诉自己我是全国最幸福的小孩，我真的很幸福。"

"哦，你能帮我吗？我有一个小儿子整天哭。他要什么，我就给什么，他还是感到不幸福。我想请你给他唱歌，告诉他你的秘诀。你是一个很勇敢的小男孩。"陌生人请求道。

布鲁点点头。"等我把柴带回家后我就来。爸爸回来的时候我们就有柴取暖了。我

⑤ porridge /'pɒrɪdʒ/ n. 稀饭

⑥ chirp /tʃɜːp/ v. 唧唧喳喳

⑦ plead /pliːd/ v. 请求

The stranger took Blue to a big cottage in the forest. In a beautiful room lay a sick boy on a silken[8] couch. His eyes were red as he had been crying. He looked angrily at his father and stared at Blue. "Who are you? You look cold. Why do you smile?"

The father took his son's hands and told him how he saw Blue in the woods singing and looking happy in spite of[9] being hungry and cold.

Blue came towards the boy and asked, "Would you like me to sing you a song? If you like it then I will continue." As Blue sang, the boy smiled as he could feel that Blue sang with his heart. "What a beautiful song! " cried the boy, "Can you stay with me and teach me to sing so that I will not be sad?" "Of course, I will. My name is Blue and what's yours?" "I'm called Ping which means peace. But I am always crying and never gives my father peace." So Blue sang and taught Ping the true meaning of peace and how to be happy. Not only Blue and Ping became the best of friends but their fathers too.

Moral: Singing your blues away also means singing your troubles away. In simple terms "never let trouble troubles you."

不停地唱，我的心也打开跟着唱。我真的没有秘诀。"

陌生人把他带到森林里的一间大屋子里。漂亮的房间里，一个病男孩躺在柔软的沙发上。他的眼睛红红的，因为他刚哭过。他生气地看着爸爸，也盯着布鲁。"你是谁？你看起来很冷，为什么还笑？"

爸爸拉起儿子的手，告诉他说他看见布鲁在森林唱歌，看起来很幸福，尽管他又饿又冷。

布鲁走近男孩问："想听我给你唱一支歌吗？如果你喜欢听，我就接着唱。"布鲁唱的时候，男孩笑了，因为他能感受到布鲁是用心在唱。"多好听的歌！"男孩叫道，"你能和我呆在一起教我唱歌吗？那样我就不伤心了。""当然可以，我叫布鲁，你呢？""我叫平，意思是和平，但我总是哭，从不让我爸爸安宁。"于是布鲁唱歌，告诉平和平的真正含义，并教他怎样才会幸福。不仅布鲁和平成了最好的朋友，他们的爸爸也成了最好的朋友。

寓意：唱走悲伤，也唱走烦恼。简单地说就是"不让烦恼靠近你"。

⑧ silken
/'sɪlkən/
adj. 柔软的
⑨ in spite of
不顾，不管

The old well

古 井

He looked back at the well, sitting alone in the bush and it made him fel sad, too.

他回头看了看古井，看到它孤零零地躺在丛林中，这使他也感到很伤心。

For months I would stop at the old well. It sat at the intersection[1] at the end of Main Road. It had been there for a hundred years. It sat under a big tree and was made of big square bluestone bricks. There was no hole in the ground anymore; it had been <u>boarded up</u>[2]. But the well was sort of special. It had a plaque[3] on it that read: This well marks the spot where the first settlers stopped for water. They found bore water here in June 1856. From this time on, the town of Kynetin was born.

I grew up in this town, just like my parents and their parents and their parents. As a country town, Kynetin's OK. Not too busy and not too quiet.

On my way home from school I would sit by the old well and watch the traffic. It helped me think. If I had a problem I would sit with my back up against the side of the well and stretch my legs out in the leaves and twigs[4] that had fallen from the tree. No one could see me and I felt the well was a special place that no one knew about.

One day, I was heading to the well as usual. When I got there it was gone! I couldn't believe it.

All that was left was a rough circle of dirt where it had stood.

At first I was furious. I threw my bag down and yelled, "Where's the well?!"

A council worker was clearing behind the tree.

"The well!" he replied. "Oh, that old thing's gone. Was taken

一连几个月我都会在古井那儿逗留一会。古井位于主路尽头的相交地段[1]，已经有100年了。它在一棵大树底下，由大块的蓝色方砖砌成，地上没有洞，因为已经被覆盖[2]住了。但是这口古井很特别，上面有一块饰板[3]写着：这口井所处的位置是第一批定居者停下来饮水的地方。1856年6月他们在这儿发现了地下水，从那以后，Kynetin镇诞生了。

像我的祖祖辈辈一样，我也是在这个乡镇长大的。Kynetin这个乡镇还不错，既不太繁忙也不太沉寂。

放学回家时，我会坐在古井旁边注视着来来往往的车辆，陷入沉思。如果有什么心事，我就会背靠着古井坐着，伸开腿放在落叶和枯枝[4]上。没有人能看到我，我觉得古井是一个没有人知道的特殊的地方。

一天，我像往常一样向古井走去。

当我到那儿时，它不见了。

我无法相信。

留下的只是围在周围的一圈泥土。

刚开始，我满腔愤怒，扔下书包大声叫道："井哪去了?!"

一个市议会议员从树后走出来。

"井吗?"他答道，"哦，古井不见了。今天下午被挪走了。关于这个地方，议会有

---

① intersection /ˌɪntəˈsekʃən/ n. 交汇，交错

② board up 覆盖

③ plaque /plɑːk/ n. 饰板

④ twig /twɪg/ n. 细枝

away this afternoon. The council's got big plans for this spot. The tree's going to be removed next week."

"What?" I gasped. "Are you mad?"

"It's only an old well," he grumbled[5]. "No use getting angry with me. Anyway, it's been moved to the bush land behind the wrecker's yard."

I rushed home. "Do you know what's happened to the old well?" I yelled at my sisters.

They just shrugged their shoulders and kept watching TV.

I flew into the kitchen to tell Mum and Dad.

"Yes, we know," said Dad.
"Yes, dear," soothed[6] Mum. "The council's been planning this for months. It's only an old well. It was dirty and needed work on it. No one's going to miss it."

"That's for sure," he agreed and they both laughed.
"Well, I will!" I screamed to their surprise and stamped[7] to my room.

I had to do something, but what? I lay on my bed and thought really hard. The next morning I had a plan. After school I went to the high school and asked to see the history professor.

My older sisters told me about him. He was old, I mean, really old. They said he was at least one hundred. No one ever went into

更大的规划。下星期这棵树也要被移走。"

"什么?"我喘着气说, "你们疯了吗?"

"只不过是一口古井。"他满怀怨言, "用不着和我生气, 不管怎样, 它已经被移到拖车院子后的丛林里了。"

我飞快地跑回家。

"你们知道古井怎么了吗?"我对姐姐们大声叫道。

她们只是耸耸肩, 继续看电视。

我跑到厨房告诉爸爸妈妈。

"是的, 我们知道了。"爸爸说。

"是的, 亲爱的。"妈妈平静地说, "议会已经为这个计划讨论了几个月了。它只是一口古井, 很脏, 还需要修理, 没有人会怀念它的。"

"那是当然。"爸爸表示同意, 两个人都笑了。

"但是我会!"我的尖叫声使他们吃了一惊, 然后我冲进我的房间。

我必须要做点什么, 但是做什么呢?

我躺在床上, 使劲地想。

第二天早上, 我想出了一个计划。

放学后, 我去高中见历史教授。

我的姐姐们和我说过这个人。他年纪大了, 我是说很老了, 他们说他至少已经100岁了。没有人去他的办公室, 因为到处是旧书、灰尘, 而且很吓人。

⑤ grumble
/'grʌmbl/
v. 发牢骚, 抱怨
⑥ sooth /suːθ/
v. 平静地说
⑦ stamp /stæmp/
v. 冲进

his office because it was full of old books and dust and was too scary.

I had no choice. I knocked gently on the door and a gruff voice barked at me. I opened it slowly and it creaked[8] loudly.

"Yeeesss," a voice spoke. It sounded just like the door. "Can I help?"

I knew what my sisters meant. There were bookshelves lining every wall, from the floor to the ceiling. They were completely packed with books and completely covered with dust!

I tried to walk in, but there were papers and books all over the floor.
"Oh, sorry about the mess," the professor said. "Don't know how it happens, but things just get everywhere."

He cleared a path for me.
"Now," he said, "I don't get visitors very often."
"Umm," I hesitated, "I've come to ask for your help."
I told him about the well and what had happened.

"Hmm," he rubbed his chin thoughtfully. "If I remember properly that well has a lot of historical importance. It should remain in the town."

"Well, we need to find out more about the well. We need to see how important it really is. I can do that," he leapt out of his chair and opened a filing cabinet. Dust clouded the air.

我没有别的办法。

我轻轻地敲了敲门，听到一个粗鲁的声音应了一声。

我慢慢地推开门，门嘎吱嘎吱地响。

"谁呀？"一个声音说，就像门发出的嘎吱的声音，"有事吗？"

我终于明白姐姐所讲的了。

每一面墙上都挂着书架，从地板到天花板，到处都是落满尘土的书。

我想走进去，但是论文和书本铺得满地都是。

"哦，不好意思，"教授说道，"不知道怎么弄的，到处都是东西。"

他清理了一条路出来。

"现在，"他说，"我没什么客人。"

"呃，"我犹豫了一下说，"我是来寻求帮助的。"

我告诉他关于古井的事。

"呃，"他摸摸下巴沉思道，"如果记得不错的话，那口古井很有历史价值，它应该继续留在镇上。"

"我们需要找到更多关于古井的历史，需要了解它是多么重要，我能做这些事。"他跳下椅子，打开一个文件柜，灰尘也随之落下。

他站起来，直盯着我。

❽ **creak** /kriːk/
v. 嘎吱

He stood up and looked directly at me. "You can get a petition together," he suggested. "If enough people signed it, the council will be forced to put it back. What do you think?"

I smiled at him. "I think that's a great idea!" I laughed.

The next day was Saturday. I sat outside the supermarket and asked everyone to sign my petition. At first many people didn't remember the old well. When I reminded them of it, they agreed that it was a shame to lose something that was a direct link to their past.

"It's irreplaceable[9]!" I announced as people gave me their signatures.

I did this every day and by the end of the week I had collected over one hundred names.

I rushed to show the professor. I thought he would be really pleased. He had been gathering information about the well. We were going to convince the council to put it back. However, when I saw his face I knew something was wrong.

"It's the well," he said. "They took it away to build a truck stop. The council's one hundred percent behind it. The Major, Mr. Simpkin, said it's going to bring thousands of dollars into the town. I don't think they're going to listen to an old professor and a kid. Simpkin is a powerful man. He's very rich and lots of people listen to him." He slumped in his chair.

"But we can't give up," I cried banging my hands on his

"你们可以联名请愿。"他建议说，"如果有很多人签名，市议会就不得不撤消计划的，你觉得怎么样？"

我笑了笑。

"真是个好注意。"我笑着说。

第二天是星期六，我站在超市外面请每个人在我的请愿书上签名。开始人们并不记得那口古井，当我告诉他们时，他们都说抛弃过去见证历史的东西真是可耻。

"它是不可取代的！"当人们签名时，我宣传道。

我每天都这样做，这个周末我已经收集了 100 多个签名。

我迫不及待地拿去给教授看。我以为他会很高兴的，因为他已经收集了关于古井的材料，我们可以说服议会撤消决定了。但是当我看到他的脸色时，我知道出事了。

"是古井，"他说，"他们移走了古井是想建一个停车场，议会 100%通过。市长 Simpkin 说这会给乡镇带来几千美元的收益。我认为他们不会听一个老教授和一个孩子的话。Simpkin 是个权力很大的人，他很有钱，很多人都听他的。他一屁股坐到椅子上。

"但是我们不能放弃。"我拍着桌子大声喊道，"我们已经做了这么多工作。"

他看着我。

❾ irreplaceable
/ˌɪrɪˈpleɪsəbl/
n. 不能替代的

desk, "Not after all the work we've done."

He looked up at me.

"Why can't we have both?" I said. "A truck stop and the well?"
"You're right," he agreed. "Tonight's the council meeting."

He leapt out of his chair and dust swirled around him, "I still have a lot of work to do. Make sure you get there early with the petition. We'll show them that they can't mess with history!" His eyes were sparkling with excitement.

In all the excitement I hadn't missed visiting the well. As I left the professor's office I realized I hadn't seen it since it'd been shifted.

I grabbed my bike and rode down Main Street, past the wrecker's yard. I reached the park and got off my bike. I walked past the trees, but couldn't see the well. It was getting dark and I would have to get to the meeting soon.

I had walked for about ten minutes then I saw it. "Oh, dear," I gasped.

It was sitting all crooked and twisted in a space between a fallen log and the old bridge. Its mortar[10] was cracked and the old bucket had been broken. Even the brass plague had been scratched. It looked very lonely.

I looked at the petition in my hands. "Just wait," I told it. "All of these people want to save you. And the professor and I are

“我们为什么不能停车场和古井两者都有呢?”我说。

“你说的对。”他说，“今晚议会召开会议。”

他跳下椅子，灰尘也随之飞舞起来。“我还有很多工作要做，你一定要带着请愿书早点到那儿，我们要告诉他们不能破坏历史!”

他的眼里闪烁着兴奋。

在兴奋之中我没有忘记去看那口古井。当我离开教授的办公室时，我意识到自从它被挪走之后我再也没有看到它了。

我抓过自行车，飞驰在主路上，经过拖车院子。到了公园后我下了车，穿过树丛，但是没看到古井，天已黑了，我应该要尽快赶到会场。

走了大约 10 分钟后，我看到了古井。

“哦，天哪!”我吸了一口气说。

它歪歪斜斜地躺在倒下的木头和古桥之间，臼已经折断，吊桶也破裂了，连黄铜色饰板也被刮掉了，它看起来那么孤单。

我看了看手上的请愿书。

“等会儿，”我告诉它，“所有这些人都想挽救你，教授和我一定会让你恢复原位。”

正在那时，我听到有声响，是细枝折断的声音，还有沉重的呼吸声。

⑩ mortar
/ˈmɔːtə(r)/
n. 臼

going to make sure that you are put back where you belong."

Just then I heard something. It was twigs breaking and heavy breathing.

Through the trees I could see Mr. Simpkin coming towards me. I didn't know what he was doing or what he wanted.

Quickly, I tucked[11] the petition into my jacket and crept behind a fallen log.

He stood at the well and looked around.

How careless had I been? There was my bike leaning up against a tree. He walked over to it.

"Where are you, you little brat[12]?" he muttered under his breath. "I'll make sure you don't ruin my plans. That truck stop is going to make me a millionaire!"

I moved back slowly and suddenly felt the most awful pain in my leg. I saw a black snake whisking[13] away.

"Snake bite," I muttered to myself. I could feel the poison rushing through my body. I had to get away from Simpkin and get help.

I stumbled[14] through the bush. My eyes became blurry[15] and my tongue swelled[16]. I was sweating a lot and I couldn't breath properly. I had not gone far when I fell down and was unable to move.

透过树丛，我看到 Simpkin 先生朝我走过来，我不知道他在干什么，或想干什么。我迅速地把请愿书塞进夹克里，悄悄地溜到放倒的木头后面。

他站在井边，朝四周看了看。

我怎么这么粗心哪！

自行车还靠在树旁，他朝它走了过去。

"你在哪儿，小家伙？"他嘀咕着说，"我不会让你打乱我的计划的，那个停车场可以使我变成一个百万富翁。"

我慢慢向后移动，突然感到腿上有一阵揪心的疼痛。

我看到一条黑蛇敏捷地溜走了。

"被蛇咬了！"我对自己说。我能感到毒液往我身上窜。

我只有离开 Simpkin 去寻求帮助。

我跌跌撞撞地穿过丛林，我的眼睛模糊了，舌头也肿了，我流了很多汗，不能正常呼吸。我还没跑多远就倒下，不能动了。

就这样，我快要死了。我感到头晕，家人的脸、古井、老教授都浮现在我的眼前。我尽力叫喊，却叫不出来。

我的脑海一片空白。

突然我听到一声重击声。光线太强了，我睁不开眼睛。

很多人在我周围跑来跑去，大喊大叫。

⑪ **tuck** /tʌk/
v. 卷起来
⑫ **brat** /bræt/
n. 小家伙
⑬ **whisk** /wɪsk/
v. 敏捷地逃走
⑭ **stumble**
/ˈstʌmbl/
v. 跌跌撞撞
⑮ **blurry** /ˈblɜːrɪ/
adj. 模糊的
⑯ **swell** /swel/
v. 发肿

This was it. I was dying. My head spun and the faces of my family, the well and the professor floated in front of my eyes. I tried to shout, but nothing came out. Everything went blank.

All of a sudden I heard a loud bang and was blinded by a terrible light. There were people all around me rushing and calling out.

"Did you see the snake?"
"What color was it?"
"We'll have to use the anti-venom[17] from Melbourne."
"Quick, everyone get moving ..."

The next thing I knew I was sitting in a hospital bed. My parents were sitting on either side of me. The professor was looking out the window and I could hear my sisters outside. They all looked worried. Their eyes were sad and Mum looked like she'd been crying.

I croaked out a "hello". They all looked up and cried with joy.

"Thank heavens," said Dad, "The doctors were able to save you. You were very lucky."

"But how?" I asked. They all looked at each other. Professor, can you tell me?" He looked at me and then at my parents. My father nodded. "It all started just after you left my office," he said. "I didn't know where you were going, but Simpkin did."

"Yes, I remember," I interrupted, "He didn't get the petition, did he?"

⑰ venom
/'venəm/
n. 毒液

"你看见蛇了吗？"

"是什么颜色的？"

"我们必须要用墨尔本岛的抗毒液。"

"快点，每个人都行动起来。"

接下来我所知道的事情就是我躺在医院的病床上了。爸爸妈妈一边一个坐在我旁边。教授看着窗外，我还可以听到我的姐姐们在外面，她们看起来很焦急，眼里含着悲伤，妈妈显然哭过。

我费力地说了一声"喂"。

他们都抬眼看，然后高兴地叫了起来。

"感谢上帝！"爸爸说，"医生们把你救活了，你真是太幸运了！"

"这是怎么事？"我问。

他们都互相看着。

"教授，你能告诉我吗？"

他看了看我，又看了看我的爸妈，爸爸点了点头。

"你离开我的办公室后，"他说，"我不知道你去了哪，但 Simpkin 知道。"

"是的，我记起来了。"我打断他说，"他没有拿到请愿书吗？"

"是 Simpkin 先生把你送到这里来的，他救了你的命。"

我看看所有的人。

这是真的。

"It was Mr. Simpkin who brought you in here. He saved your life."

I looked at them all. It was true.

Mr. Simpkin had seen me stumble away. At first he was going to try and scare me off. He wanted to get the petition and tear it into pieces. However, when he saw me lying on the ground something occurred to him.

He looked back at the well, sitting alone in the bush and it made him feel sad, too. He used to throw stones down it when he was a kid. Once he remembered saving a cat that had fallen down it.

He carried me to his car and took me straight to hospital. He stayed with me until my parents arrived. This meant that he was late for the meeting and that he might have lost the truck stop.

When he reached the council offices he told them what had happened. He handed them the petition. He suggested they consider putting back the well and offered to move the truck stop somewhere else.

At first everyone was dumbfounded. Here was the most powerful man in town covered in dirt; his face smeared[18] with mud, telling them he'd changed his mind! He hadn't realised how popular the well was. He remembered when things are with us all the time we mustn't take them for granted. That studying the past is as important as planning for the future. He couldn't believe that one little kid could affect so many people's minds.

⑱ smear
/smɪə(r)/
v. 涂, 粘

Simpkin 看到我跌跌撞撞跑开了。最初他想把我吓走，他想拿到请愿书后把它撕碎，但是看到我躺在地上，他改变了想法。

他回头看了看古井，看到它孤零零地躺在丛林中，这使他也感到很伤心。他小的时候也经常往里面扔石头，他还记得曾经救起过一只掉在里面的猫。

他把我抱上车，直接送我到医院。在我父母赶来之前，他一直陪在我身边。这意味着那天的会议他迟到了，可能他的停车场计划也泡汤了。

当他到达议会办公室后，他告诉他们所发生的事情。他把请愿书递给他们，建议他们考虑把井放回原处，把停车场建在其他地方。

起初，每个人都惊呆了。这个城镇里最有影响的人，浑身是土，脸上还有泥，告诉他们说他改变主意了。以前，他没有意识到古井是多么深入人心。现在，他记起来了，我们不该对一直都在我们身边的事物视而不见，研究过去和规划未来一样重要。他不相信一个小孩能够影响这么多人的想法。

这就是古井的故事，它不仅是我的古井，也是属于大家的古井。

我依然经常去坐在它旁边，但有时我会有同伴一起去。一个叫 Joe Simpkin 的人和我

And that's the story of the old well. Only it's not my well, it belongs to everybody.

I still go and sit near it, but sometimes I have company. A man called Joe Simpkin and I sit together with our backs against the wall and our feet outstretched under the tree. He shares stories with me about the things he used to do when he was a kid growing up in this country town.

一起坐在树下，背靠着墙，双脚伸开，他给
我讲述在这城镇他小时候的故事。

图书在版编目（CIP）数据

英汉对照·心灵阅读. 6，情操篇/陈爱明，李小艳编译. —北京：外文出版社，2004
ISBN 7－119－03730－7

Ⅰ. 英… Ⅱ.①陈…②李… Ⅲ. 英语－对照读物－英、汉 Ⅳ. H319.4

中国版本图书馆 CIP 数据核字（2004）第 057282 号

> 外文出版社网址：
> http://www.flp.com.cn
> 外文出版社电子信箱：
> info@flp.com.cn
> sales@flp.com.cn

英汉对照·心灵阅读（六）

情 操 篇

编　译　陈爱明　李小艳
审　校　林　立

责任编辑　王　蕊　李春英
封面设计　时振晓
印刷监制　张国祥
出版发行　外文出版社
社　址　北京市百万庄大街 24 号　　邮政编码　100037
电　话　（010）68995963/5883（编辑部）
　　　　（010）68329514/68327211（推广发行部）
印　刷　北京中印联印务有限公司
经　销　新华书店/外文书店
开　本　大 32 开　　　　　字　数　150 千字
印　数　10001－15000 册　　印　张　8.375
版　次　2006 年 1 月第 1 版第 2 次印刷
装　别　平
书　号　ISBN 7－119－03730－7/H·1617（外）
定　价　15.80 元